Those Amazing Coins
A Kid's Guide to Collecting

BY KEVIN FLYNN, RON VOLPE,
AND KELSEY FLYNN

First Edition 2000

Published by
BGCS
8725 4th Ave
Brooklyn, NY 11209

Acknowledgment

We would like to thank Kenneth Bressett for writing the foreword for this book. Ken has been helping the hobby for years by sharing information and teaching others. He is a leader who does by his actions so that others will follow and learn.

We would like to thank Toni Bocciti, Melissa Bocciti, Matthew Flynn, and Kelsey Flynn for helping with the front cover. We would like to thank Melissa Bocciti for writing a section for the book.

We would like to thank J.T. Stanton, Bill Fivaz, Sam Lukes, John Wexler, Alan Meghrig, Bill Van Note, William Afanato, Jim Lafferty, Craig Sholley, Tony Boccuti, John Bordner, William Murray Jr., Bruce Hickmott, Roderick Gaddy, and Brian Raines for supplying some of the coins and/or information for this book. These individuals are always willing to lend a hand when needed and do so for the benefit of the hobby.

We would like to thank Beth Deisher of Coin World; Dave Harper of Numismatic News; Mike Gumpel, Rudy Bahr, Gail Baker, Kelly Swett, Robert Hoge, and Stephen Bobbitt of the American Numismatic Association; and the United States Mint for its help with the Washington State Quarters and other information.

We would like to thank Mrs. Croker and her fourth-grade class for reviewing this book and offering their comments. We would especially like to thank Veran Drenik for the art work and editing she provided. We would like to thank Donna Brophy for editing.

Table of Contents

Acknowledgments   3
Foreword   5
Introduction   7
Basics of Coins and Money   10
Handling and Examining Coins   16
Storing Coins   19
How to Start a Coin Collection   25
From a Kid's View by Kelsey Flynn   30
Hunting for the New and Old by Melissa Bocciti   33
Washington State Quarters   37
Sacagawea Dollar   55
Modern Series of United States Coins   59
Other Collectible Series   76
Grading Coins   90
Buying Coins   95
Collecting Die Varieties   97
Collecting Error Coins   102
Collecting Foreign Coins   104
Collecting Hobo Nickels   106
Collecting Ancient Coins   108
Conclusion   112
Terms and Definitions   113
Recommended Readings   115
Bibliography   117
NCADD Membership Applications   118
ANA Membership Application   119
Hobo Nickel Membership Application   120

Foreword by Kenneth Bressett

I have had an interest in collecting coins for more than sixty years. When I started looking for coins in my change, it was easy to find just about every date and mintmark for everything as far back as 1892. It was exciting to find any coin worth more than face value, but the real thrill was to complete each set or trade with others for missing pieces.

Collecting coins is different today. Nearly all of those really old coins are gone from circulation and it is unusual to find anything dated before 1965 when silver was in daily use. Yet it is still possible to have fun searching for old coins and filling sets of different dates and mintmarks and is just as rewarding now as it has ever been. It is the fulfillment of a challenge that makes it so much fun.

This book has been written for a young beginner. It has in it everything needed for a child to get started and to continue on for years of enjoyment. It is exactly the kind of book I wanted when I started collecting; unfortunately, there were no such books back then.

The great value of this book is that it gives clear answers to all of the questions that any beginner needs to know. It is written in a style that is easy to understand, and it emphasizes the enjoyment and fun of coin collecting. Best of all, it has been written by both an expert on the subject and his young daughter, who is equally enthusiastic about the hobby.

You will learn a lot about coins in this book. You will also learn about the history of this great country, the artistry of designs used on American money, the different kinds of metals used in these coins, and how to appreciate the value of these rare and unusual treasures that so often pass unnoticed through the hands of the general public. It may well be the beginning of an adventure that will last for the rest of your life. I hope that it is and that you enjoy your excursion into coin collecting as much as I have.

Kenneth Bressett
Past President
American Numismatic Association
November 1999

Introduction

Coin collecting is one of the oldest hobbies in the world. People have been collecting coins since coins were first created about 2700 years ago. In ancient times many coins had the picture of the current leader or important battles or events. Besides being used for buying and trading they were used to communicate news across the land. The two photos below on the left are of Julius Ceasar and was made around 46 to 47 BC, making this coin more than 2000 years old. The two photos to the right are of Hadrian and was made between 119 and 138 AD or about 1900 years ago.

Today, in almost every country, people of all ages enjoy collecting coins from their own country and from other countries. Here in the United States, there are about 5 million people who collect coins.

Can anyone collect coins? Of course. If you like to save coins from your pocket change, coins from around the world, or have been given coins from a relative, you are on your way to enjoying this hobby. How should you start collecting coins? There are thousands of ways to collect coins and there is no right or wrong way to do it. All you need to do is begin by collecting what you like best.

Some people collect coins from different countries to show where they have been or to show where they would like to go. Imagine having one coin from each country in the world. Other people collect coins because they like the image (picture) on the coin.

Some people collect coins because they are rare and worth alot of money. There are some real exciting and rare coins out there. Below, on the left, is a 1913 Liberty Nickel, one of only five made. This coin sold for more than a million dollars. The photo on the right is of an 1804 Dollar. This coin sold for more than four million dollars, the most ever paid for a single coin.

**Photo courtesy of
Spectrum Coins**

**Photo by Douglas Plasencia
Courtesy of Bowers & Merena**

Putting together a coin collection can be fun and challenging. Coins can also teach us about the history of a country at the time the coin was made. The image on most coins are of famous people or important events. For example, the two photos below on the left are of the Eisenhower Dollar with President Eisenhower on the front, and on the back is a picture representing the moon landing. The two photos below on the right are of the Indian cent struck between 1859 and 1909 and are symbolic of the American West during that time.

Coins come in many different shapes and sizes including round, square, and even triangles. They are also made of different metals including gold, silver, and copper.

Imagine holding a coin from the time of the American Civil War in the 1860s, or the Revolutionary War around 1776, or back to the time of Columbus. It is amazing that a simple little coin could have traveled through all that time. Just think of how many different people may have held that coin, maybe a president, a king, a queen, or even a famous athlete.

Remember, the most important thing, is that coin collecting is a hobby. It's something you do for enjoyment and fun. It's also a good way to meet new friends who enjoy collecting and share what you have learned or found. There are coin shows, stores, clubs, chat sites on the internet, and other ways to view coins or meet people who enjoy collecting. There is also a chance you can make money in this hobby, but first collect coins because you enjoy them.

Basics of Coins and Money

We use money to buy things that we need or want. Adults earn money by working. They go to the store and buy food with money. They use money to buy clothes, furniture, books, a car, and many other things. But why do we need money? Isn't there another way to get the things we need? What was used before money was created?

Before money, people used to trade for goods. One example of this is let's say you are a farmer and you needed seeds to plant your crops. In town there is a store that has seeds. You could take something of value to the store that the store needs, let's say chickens, and trade them for seeds.

What would happen if the store did not need the chickens, and the farmer did not have anything else to trade? How would he get the seeds? Let's think about how it would work today. Say, one of your parents is a police officer. How would they trade for food or clothes if there was not any money?

These are the reasons why we use money. It is the way we can give an item value so we can buy or sell it. For example, a farmer's chickens are worth $20.00 and one bag of seeds is worth $15.00. By giving each item a value, we are now able to trade them using money. Plus, because money is used by everyone, the farmer can sell the chickens for money and use the money to buy the things he needs.

Now, the farmer can take the chickens to a different store that wants the chickens. The store owner pays the farmer money for the chickens. The farmer can then use the money to buy seeds. For our parent, the police officer, they are paid money for doing their job. Our parent can then use the money to buy things that are needed for the family such as food and clothing.

Who is in charge of making money? The government of each country is in charge of the money used in that country. The United States Government decides what "*legal tender*" is used here in the United States. The legal tender is the value of the coin or paper money.

The value is also known as the "*face value,*" or "*denomination.*" All of these tell us how much a coin or paper money is worth. For example, one dollar is worth 100 cents. The value of the metal used in making the coin is called the "*intrinsic value.*" For example, the intrinsic value of the metal in the Washington Quarter is about 3 cents, where the face value is 25 cents. For the American Eagle fifty-dollar gold piece, the intrinsic value is about $325.00, where the face value is $50.00. This is because gold is very valuable.

Where is the money made? Today, in the United States, coins and money are made at the United States Mint in Philadelphia and two branch mints, Denver and San Francisco. Several other branch mints were used in the past. To tell which mint a coin was made (struck) at, a mintmark is placed on the coins. The following mintmarks were used for the eight United States mints used for striking coins: "C" for Charlotte, "CC" for Carson City, "D" for Dahlonega, "D" for Denver, "O" for New Orleans, "P" for Philadelphia, "S" for San Francisco, and "W" for West Point.

There are different types of money made at the Mint. Business strikes are coins that will used by the public to buy and sell things. Each year billions of coins are made for general usage. Each coin is struck once in the coining press. Then the coins are dumped into bins with millions of others of the same denomination. Then the coins are sent out to banks so we can use them to buy the items we want.

Some coins are made especially for collectors. These coins are sold as Mint Sets or special sets. These sets contain one of each denomination from each Mint where the coin was produced. So if the cent, nickel, dime, quarter, and half dollar are being struck at both the Philadelphia and Denver Mints for a year, the Mint Set would contain 10 coins, one of each denomination from each Mint. These coins are struck once like business strikes from normal dies, but after they are struck, they are placed into the sets. They are not dumped into bins where they would come in contact with other coins. On the top left of the next page is a photo of a 1991 Mint Set. On the top right of the next page is a photo of a 1996 Mint Set.

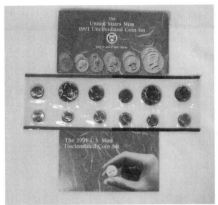 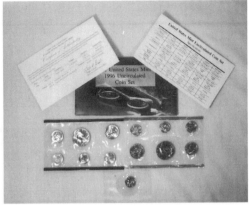

Proof coins are also made for collectors. These coins are made from special dies that are highly polished to give the coins mirrorlike surface. Proof coins are struck twice to make the design really sharp. After each coin is struck it is placed by hand into a set, so there are no "*bag marks*".

When coins are placed with other coins, they can bang into each other causing marks and nicks. This does not happen with proof coins. The same design is used for business strikes and proofs for each denomination. There are Lincoln cent business strikes and Lincoln cent proofs. Proof coins are sold in sets that are sold by the Mint or coin dealers.

Each proof set contains one of each denomination that is made at the Mint. Each coin in a regular proof set is made of the same metal as the business strike. A special silver proof set is also made in which the dime, quarter, and half dollar are made of silver instead of the normal clad copper nickel. Prestige sets are also made and contain commemorative coins struck in that year. On the top left of the next page is a 1997 proof set. On the right of the next page is a 1992 proof set. Today, proof coins are only struck at the San Francisco Mint.

Commemorative coins are made to honor a person or special event. These coins are made in limited numbers and not made for regular circulation. Sometimes commemorative coins are created to help pay for monuments or special events. Below is a 1996 Olympic Game Commemorative Proof Half Dollar.

Obverse   Reverse

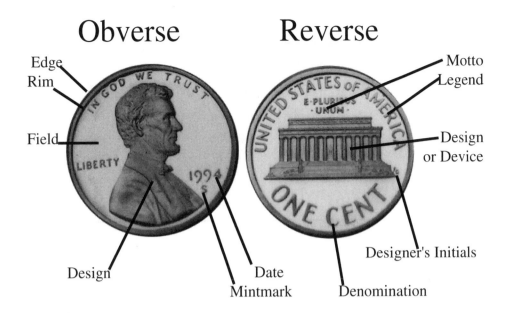

Edge
Rim
Field
Design   Date
          Mintmark

Motto
Legend
Design or Device
Designer's Initials
Denomination

Obverse - Front of the coin.

Reverse - Back of the coin.

Date - The year the coin was struck.

Mintmark - Tells us which Mint a coin was struck, for example: P stands for Philadelphia, D for Denver, and S for San Francisco.

Design - The main image on the coin. For example, on the Lincoln cent, the main image on the obverse would be the image of President Lincoln. On the reverse, it would be the Lincoln Memorial.

Device - Same as the main design on the coin.

Legend - The words "UNITED STATES OF AMERICA," which are required to be on all coins struck at the United States Mint.

Motto - The words "E PLURIBUS UNUM," which are required to be on all coins today. This is Latin for "*ONE OUT OF MANY.*"

Rim - This is the outer raised portion of the coin.

Edge - The side of the coin.

Field - The flat surface of the coin.

Designer's Initials - Initials of the person who created the design.

Denomination - The value assigned to the coins. Also known as the face value and also the legal tender.

Handling and Examining Coins

It is very important to always handle coins with care. If coins are handled incorrectly, they can be ruined forever. A few simple rules will help keep your coins in the best condition. Handle your coins as little as possible. If you have to pick up your coin, hold it only by the edges. **Never touch the front (obverse) or back (reverse) of the coin.** Even putting your coin in the palm of your hand can damage a coin. Our skin has oil, plus if there is any dirt on your hands, it can get on the coin. Never handle coins when your hands are dirty. Try to wash your hands before handling coins and make sure they are dry. You could also wear cotton gloves to be completely safe.

Do not eat or drink while examining your coins. If you have to cough or sneeze, put the coin down and turn your head. Try not to talk or breath on the coin, because even vapor can affect the surface of the coin.

If you want to hold the coin to examine it, hold the coin between your thumb and index finger. Make sure you keep a soft mat on the table under the coin in case it falls. The condition of a coin has a great deal to do with its value. If a coin is dented, scratched, tarnished, or has ugly fingerprints on it, it will be far less valuable.

Do not attempt to clean a coin. If a coin shows signs of cleaning, it is worth far less. There are ways to remove some dirt using soap and water, but this should be left to the experts. It's not worth possibly damaging your coins. Once a coin is cleaned it cannot be restored to its original condition. In the photo on the top left of the next page, the coin is first placed on a protective holder, then examined. In the photo on the right, the coin is being held between the thumb and index finger while being examined.

When examining a coin, it is important to use good lighting. Without good lighting, it is hard to see if a coin has been damaged. It is important to examine all parts of the coin. The value of the coin mainly depends on the condition of the coin. For circulated coins, the amount of wear is the most important part in determining condition. For Mint State coins or coins that have no signs of wear from circulation, the number of marks, scratches, contact marks, nicks, color, and eye appeal are all important. Good lighting is needed to see these flaws. Remember, a small difference in the condition of the coin can have a big difference in the value of the coin.

A strong light is recommended for viewing your coin. Halogen lights are very good. Having a lamp that can be moved around or tilted can be very helpful as you can change the amount of light and not have to move the coin themselves. Hold the coin about 2 to 3 feet from the light. When examining the coin, tilt the coin at an angle so that the light reflects from the coin's surface to your eye. Tilt and turn the coin so that different parts of the coin can be observed.

To look at a coin real closely, a magnifying glass is used. A magnifying glass is a glass that makes an object look larger. The power of the magnifying glass means how big the object is when you look through it. A magnifying glass that is 2x (x relates to the power) means that an object looks 2 times its normal size. A 10x magnifying glass makes an object look 10 times its normal size. There are many different types of magnifying glasses. They come in different shapes and different power levels. Some have lights attached with them. For normal coin examination a magnifying glass between 4x and 8x should be fine. For looking at very small parts of the coin, use a 10x to 16x. Some glasses are better than others because better glass is used. The coin looks much clearer through these. When buying a magnifying glass, bring a coin with you and examine it through different glasses to see which you like the best. One of the most popular is the 5x packette, which is made by Bausch and Lomb. Below are several different magnifying glasses.

Storing Coins

It's important to properly store your coins so they do not become damaged. You should not place your coins in a bag all together or throw them in your drawer, because the coins can bang against each other and they will become nicked and scratched. Also do not store them near something that is hot, because this can damage the surface of the coin.

There are many different ways to store your coins to keep them protected. What you use depends alot on what you collect and what your goals are. For example, let's say you are trying to collect one of each date of the Lincoln cent series. There are books available specifically for storing these.

If you like to collect all types of coins and keep them together, the easiest way to store your coins is in 2" by 2" cardboard holders. These are safe for storage and because there is a plastic window, you can easily see the front and back of your coins. There are different sizes for different size coins. To insert a coin, first choose a holder where the window is the same size as the coin. Lay the holder flat, place the coin on top in the middle, fold over the holder, and staple it shut. When you staple, it is best to staple around the four sides. Make sure you do not accidently staple your coin.

Once you have your coins in these holders, you can put the coins in boxes or in vinyl pages where you can put up to 20 coins in a page. These pages fit into a three ring binder and allow you to enjoy your coins in a book format. The photo on the top left of the next page shows different size cardboard holders. The photo on the right shows different albums that can hold these 2" by 2" cardboard holders. If you want, you can use smaller holders, so you can bring them to coin shows or a friend's house. With your larger book, you can set it up any way you want. For example, have Lincoln cents on one page, Jefferson nickels on another.

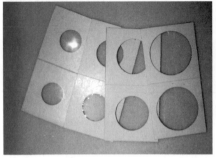 

Another nice thing about cardboard holders is that you can write notes on them. For example, you could write when you bought the coin, how much you paid, or anything special you like about the coin. Make sure you also flatten down the staples so that they do not scratch other coins. Also, when taking coins out of a cardboard holder, make sure not to scratch the coin on a staple.

There are several other ways of storing single coins. Flips are clear plastic envelopes with two pockets. These can be used to display two coins, or a single coin with a description of the coin or any other information. Flips are made of vinyl, which is soft and easy to use, but not recommended for long-term storage because the oil in the vinyl can cause damage to the coins over long-term storage. Flips are also made of a different material that is safer but more expensive. These flips are of a stiffer material since the oil is removed from the vinyl to avoid damage over a long-term. Make sure you ask when you buy flips if they are safe for long-term storage.

Paper envelopes can be used as an inexpensive storage method. They are inexpensive; however, you have to remove the coin to view them. You can also write any notes on the outside of these envelopes. On the top left of the next page is a 2-inch flip. The front pocket contains a coin, and the back is used to hold an insert with a description. On the right is a paper envelope holder.

The problem with a cardboard holder, flip, or paper holder is that the coin can still be damaged if it is dropped or banged into other coins. Hard plastic holders do not have this problem. Some of these also have the benefit of an air-tight seal. This is important because air can change the color of the coin. With hard plastic holders you get to see both sides of the coin, the coin is protected, and you can use stickers to put notes on the holders. Below on the left is a snap-together plastic holder. Below in the middle is a holder that is screwed together.

There are also holders you can get that hold all denominations for a given year. This would be useful if you want to store one of each proof coin for a year. Below on the right are two different sets that hold each denomination. These holders are also good protection if the set is dropped, and some are air tight.

If you want to collect all the coins of a series, the most affordable way is to use coin folders. These are easy to use and a good way to start. These folders provide a space for each coin made for general use, including all dates and mintmarks. But, only one side of the coin can be seen. One problem is that there is no plastic protection for the front and back of the coin. When you put coins into the folder's holes, you may have to use a little muscle. The holes are made small so the coins will not fall out. If you are having a little trouble, try to put the top of the coin in first, then the bottom. Below is a folder for the Jefferson nickel series. Coin folders can be bought for almost any United States coin series.

If you are collecting a complete set of each date and mintmark for a single series and you want good protection for your coins, coin albums are the best choice if you can afford it. Remember as you start out, you have to keep to your budget. But as you save your allowance, maybe you can get a nicer album to save your coins. Coin albums are attractive books in which both sides of the coins can be viewed. There is a removable plastic slide to protect both sides of the coin, and these albums are probably the best and safest way to store your coins. When removing or inserting coins from these albums, make sure you use a glove, cloth, or piece of plastic so that you do not damage the coin. Do not push on the front or back of the coin with your bare finger. Below are different types of coin albums made for an entire series of coins.

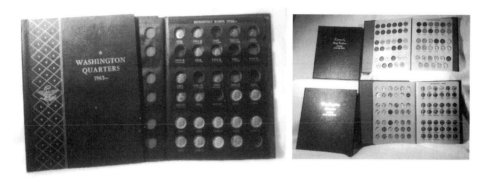

It is important when placing or removing the coin in a folder or album not to touch the front or back of the coin. First, holding the coins by the edge between your thumb and index finger, place the coin over top of the place you are going to place it in the album.

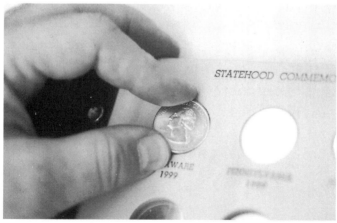

Second, use either a cardboard holder or cloth to place over the coin. With the cardboard holder, you can see the coin easily. With the thumb and index finger, push down on the rim of the coin. Make sure the coin is even, not one side down further than the other. This is because air pockets might form around the coin.

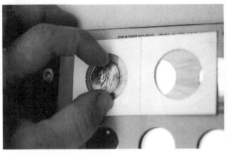 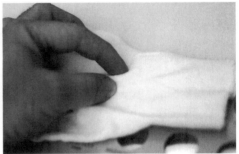

Another way to store coins is in tubes. These are great for extra coins that are not very expensive. The tubes allow you to store many of your coins together. Tubes are clear rolls for coins.

Make sure your coins are stored in a safe place. They should not be near heat or moisture or a place where the temperature changes alot. Usually you can store them in a desk or dresser drawer as long as it is not too close to a window or radiator.

There are many places to buy coins and accessories. You can try your local coin dealer or a coin show. If there aren't any nearby, try mail order. Check the classified ads in a coin paper or magazine to buy or sell coins or equipment. Most places are reputable and the editors do watch out for bad business, but be sure you can always check with the complaint department.

How to Start a Coin Collection

There are so many different ways to collect coins. You could collect coins found in your pocket change. You could collect one of each denomination from the year you were born or the year your parents were born. If you really like one type or series like the Lincoln cents, you could collect one of each date the coin was made, or even one of each date and mintmark that the coin was made.

A challenge would be to put together one of each coin from each series made in the 20th century from the year 1900 to 2000. After you have done this, you could continue with one of each coin from each series made during the 19th century between 1800 and 1900. This would include denominations that were not used in the 20th century such as the two, three, and twenty cent series shown below. Did you know that the United States Mint made these coins?

Two Cent   Three Cent Nickel   Twenty Cent

For any collection, you should start out simple and expand as you complete the set. For example, start with a date and mintmark set for each Lincoln cent from 1941 to present. After you have done this, finish up the series from 1909 through 1940.

The easiest and best way to start collecting is to collect a series that is currently being made by the Mint. These coins can be found in your pocket change. There are five different denominations currently being struck at the United States Mint. They are the Lincoln cent, Jefferson nickel, Roosevelt dime, Washington quarter, and Kennedy half dollar. These series are covered in detail in the middle of the book.

Kennedy half dollars are not used much by people, but sometimes you can find them or you can ask the teller at your local bank. Get a coin folder for each of these five series and try to collect one for each date and mintmark from 1965 to present. This is a fun and inexpensive way to start as you will not have to pay any extra for the coins and since you should be able to find these in your change. Another easy way to start a collection is to start on a modern series, which were only made for a few years. The Susan B. Anthony Dollar was only struck from 1979 to 1981 and in 1999. The Eisenhower Dollar was only struck from 1971 to 1978. Coins from these series can be bought cheaply at coin shows or shops. Your parents or grandparents also might have some. When you buy coins at stores or coin shows, make sure you talk to your parents first, and plan on how much you are going to spend. Coin collecting is a hobby; collect what you enjoy.

The new 50-state quarter program offers a great way to start collecting. These quarters can be found right in your pocket change. These new quarters are covered in detail in the next section.

Die varieties and errors are another growing part of the hobby. A brief description and some examples are given in this book. There are many books dedicated to these types of coins.

One way to add to the fun of collecting is to join a club. There are many local, regional, and national clubs for collectors and many have special programs for young coin collectors, also known as Young Numismatists or YNs. The **American Numismatic Association** (ANA) is the world's largest coin club and sponsors many events and activities for young collectors. The ANA can also tell you about the clubs and activities in your area.

The ANA sponsors many coin shows each year, including the largest coin show of the year. Each year, this main coin show is in a different part of the country and features hundreds of coin dealers and many fascinating exhibits. Above is a photograph of the 1986 ANA Coin Convention in Milwaukee, Wisconsin. (Photograph courtesy of the ANA).

The ANA holds a coin auction for young collectors each summer at its national coin show, **The World's Fair of Money** (R). You can bid on coins at the auction or, if you can't attend, you may bid through the mail. All of the auction items (or "lots") are paid for with special YN Dollars. These are earned by performing a number of fun and educational coin collecting activities, like visiting a local coin shop or giving a talk about a special coin.

The **ANA YN Treasure Trivia Game** is played by students between the ages of 6 and 18 who attend the ANA convention.

Prizes are awarded to students for following a treasure map and finding answers to trivia questions. All of the players also receive a number of collectible items - and all of this is free!

At many coin shows, there are special exhibits of really nice coins. Young collectors can exhibit their coins at the ANA shows, winning awards and full scholarships to attend a full week of "Coin Camp" in Colorado Springs, Colorado. There are also awards for writing articles or participating in **ANA's National Coin Week** activities.

The photograph above shows the opening ceremonies of the 1997 ANA Summer Seminar, held each year in Colorado Springs, Colorado. Collectors come here from all over the country to learn from some of the leading experts and to share information with others, (photograph courtesy of the ANA).

The ANA also has the largest numismatic circulating library. As a member, you can borrow books, (photograph courtesy of the ANA).

The ANA has home study courses on grading coins, understanding how coins are made, and other interesting subjects. The American Numismatic Association is there to help you learn about coins and enjoy the hobby. ANA junior membership is $11.00 a year and includes the monthly magazine "The Numismatist" and "First Strike," a special twice-a-year section for YNs.

If you or your parents have any questions or you want to join the fun at ANA, call the toll-free number 800-367-9723 and ask for the education department, or write them at American Numismatic Association, 818 North Cascade Avenue, Colorado Springs, CO 80903-3279. There is an application for membership in the back of this book.

From a Kid's View by Kelsey Flynn

Coins are very interesting and one of my favorite hobbies, although soccer is my *favorite activity*. I have two coin books, and I enjoy looking at them and showing them to my friends at school and at the pool in the summer. (But I have to be careful not to get them wet.) Most of the coins my dad gives to me, but I also look for neat coins in my pocket change.

Coins were originally used in ancient Greece and Rome as a way to buy things, but they were also used to help celebrate important events like the Olympics. Because the Greek and Roman empires were huge, the use of coins came to many other countries. You can buy some ancient Greek and Roman coins that are thousands of years old for low prices. Ancient coins are collected just like coins made today.

Coins from ship wrecks and treasures are really awesome. Imagine finding old, gold coins in *perfect* condition at the bottom of the ocean! The *S.S. Central America*, which sunk in 1857 during a violent hurricane produced gold coins valued at more than 100 million dollars, including one gold block which weighed 80 pounds.

Collecting coins from different countries is my favorite way to collect them. I have coins from almost *every* major country in the world! Some of these I got from friends and family members who were in other countries and brought some coins back for me. Some I bought at coin shows when I was with my dad. While he's looking for coins that he likes, I search for stuff that I like or don't have. But you don't just have to collect *coins*. You can also collect foreign bills ranging in value anywhere from $1.00 to $1000.00!

One of my books is a Lincoln Cents (penny) book. Did you know that in 1943, copper was needed for World War II, so pennies were made of steel? You won't find any of these pennies in your change, but your parents or grandparents might have some, or you can usually find them at coin shows.

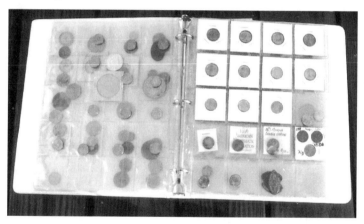

My other book (which is shown above) is any random coins I find or dad gives me that I like. I like soccer. So, I have an Olympics commemorative soccer coin from 1996 (*girls* soccer). Some of my other favorites are: Silver Dollars, Mercury Dimes, and State Quarters.

State Quarters are a good place to start collecting these days. Collecting these coins is my second favorite way to collect. I enjoy collecting State Quarters because it's fun to search for them in your change and you can find them at stores and banks, (for the same amount they're worth, like trading). When my family went on vacation to the shore, I went food shopping with Dad and we received some new quarters in our change. We asked at the front if any rolls of quarters were available and we were able to buy a roll of the new Georgia quarters for the face value.

One of the nice things about the new state quarters is that each state will have a unique design for the reverse. As you may already know, only five state quarters will come out each year for a 10 year period, and they will be released in the order the state became part of the United States. For the year 1999, the states were: Delaware, Pennsylvania, New Jersey, Connecticut, and Georgia. Dad got me a set of proof quarters for my 10th birthday which contained one of each of the 5 state quarters for 1999.

I don't have as much interest in coin shows as dad does, but I do like them. He knows lots of people at coin shows and likes talking to them and looking at coins. Some coins at shows are pretty expensive, but there are alot of less expensive coins that I can afford for my sets. Most coin dealers are very helpful, but sometimes they are busy. Don't be afraid to ask a question, but remember to be patient and polite. My dad's favorite type of coin to collect are coins with errors. Sometimes he forgets and thinks they're my favorite too!

Sometimes at coin shows, I get to see other types of collectibles. At a recent show, there were two tables with Pokemon Cards so you would be able to see them there. (If you like them, I'm not crazy about Pokemon Cards, but I do collect some.)

Coin Collecting is called "The World's Oldest Hobby", and it probably is. I think all kids can collect coins if they want to. It's easy!

Hunting for the New and Old
by Melissa Boccuti   (age 11)

I guess the first coins I ever received were in a Proof Set. They were dated 1989. I don't remember getting this set because that was when I was born. My dad got it for me. I was a coin collector then and I didn't even know it. My dad is a part-time coin dealer, so I have been around them all my life. When I was younger, I used to go with him to the coin shops in our area. I would call them the money stores.

I can remember three shows that he would go to all the time. I would sit there as he looked at all the coins. He would show me some of the neater ones now and then. This is how I learned. There were coins I had never even seen. I was used to the coins we all see now, such as the Lincolns, Jeffersons.....and so on. I knew what was out there were from school and how much each was worth. But now I was seeing coins which were still a Penny, nickel, dime, and quarter, but they didn't look anything like I had ever seen before! I knew that each coin had a date on it from the year it was made. That's called the mintage year. I was seeing coins that were VERY OLD, made back in the early 1900s and even older ones from the 1800s. I would think they had to be pretty expensive because they were so old. Some were, but as it turned out, a lot were not.

The dealers my Dad and I would visit sometimes gave me old coins. And when I got home I would ask my dad, how much it was worth. As it turned out, the Indian cent in Good condition dated 1890 was only worth about $1.00. As I grew older, I started collecting pennies. I got a Whitman folder 1959 to present, and would look for the coins I needed to fill the holes in it. Some of them were easy to find and some I could not find at all. The mintmarked coins were the hardest to find. The D (Denver) and S (San Francisco) coins were made on the west coast and I live on the east coast. So most of the coins I would look at were P mints. (Philadelphia Mint). I would look at all the pennies I could find just to fill a hole in my book. I still need a few more coins in the book to fill it all the way up, but that's what makes it fun. Each year, when the new pennies come out, my dad and I have a contest to see who can find the first coin dated for that year. I usually win. I received my first magnifier when I was 6 and it really made the coins easy to see. I still have it and use it all the time.

My dad sets up his coin cases for at least three coin shows a month. My mom and I go to two of them. I remember the first one I went to. It was a big room with I guess 30 to 40 dealers in it. All of them had tables with show cases and lamps and lots and lots of all kinds of coins. I was a little scared because I didn't know anyone and most of the people were adults there. I stayed at my dad's table and just looked around. A few times my dad asked if I would watch his table while he went to look at another dealer's coins. It was neat to be there as people came to look at what was in my dad's showcase.

As time went on, I started to wander around the room and see what was out there. So many coins. Some dealers have boxes of lower priced coins and some just have the really good stuff. That means more money. I found out that some dealers like the kids and will answer questions. They'll let me look through their boxes for coins that I need for my collection.

Most people walking around the room have a list of coins that they are looking for. They call that the want list. When I go to coin shows now I bring a list, but sometimes I bring one of my folders and try to get the coins to fill in the holes. If a dealer is busy with someone, I don't interrupt him. I'll wait or move on to a dealer who is not as busy. Then I ask him if he has any pennies or Walkers. I really like the Walking Liberty Half Dollars. Sometimes I will show the dealer my book and ask if he has any coins that I need. Being a kid, I don't have a lot of money to spend on them and some of the dealers don't carry the lower grade stuff that I need. Some dealers do though and I have been lucky to find some coins that I need. There is nothing like getting a coin and filling a hole in the book. One less to go I say with a smile.

I have a Red Book that has all the coin pictures in it and the prices. Like I said earlier, I like the Walkers. They have a nice picture of a lady (Miss Liberty) on the front and an eagle on the back. Some of the coins are expensive, but most of them I can even afford. I have a 1916, which was the first year they made them and also a 1947, which was the last year. I also have a lot of the dates and mintmarks in-between. I found that the dealers that have the lower grade coins remember me when I see them show after show. They're nice and always ask how I am doing with my collection. Most dealers know me by name now because I go there so often.

I have noticed that there are a lot more kids coming to the show in the past few years. I think with the new state quarters coming out, there will be even more. Like all kids, I have collected other things. I was into Beanie Babies and Pokemon cards, but they seemed to die out after a short time. They were neat to collect and are the same as coins in that I tried to get a full set. No one seems to care about them now. I guess you could call them a fad.

My dad tells me coin collecting has been around for a long time and that there will always be collectors of coins. With the new quarters, I can see this really being something that a kid can collect. It will take 10 years to get them all, but the best part about it is that you can find them in the change you get. A lot of the dealers at the shows carry the new quarters and the folders and maps to put them in. I have a full set so far. I couldn't find a few or the D mintmarks so I bought them at one of the shows. They're not expensive, around $0.50 for each, but they are in uncirculated condition.

The coin shows are a great place to see some really cool coins. You won't believe how many coins are there! Things like 1/2 cents and a half of a penny? Yep, they made them and other weird coins like three cent coins and twenty cent coins. I don't have any of them, but they sure are cool. There are even gold coins at the shows, small one to big ones. Nope, don't have any of them yet either but someday I will. I want to finish my Walker set and then move on to maybe the Buffalo Nickels. That coin has an Indian and a Buffalo on it. Most of the dates for those are cheap. In the Red Book, there are alot of prices under $1.00 each in the lower grades.

My favorite coin is the three leg Buffalo Nickel. Sometimes I see a boy who goes to school with me at these shows. He and his dad collect coins, too. Sometimes we talk about the coins we have. Some of the kids in school are collecting the new quarters, too. Maybe I'll see them at the show some day. Collecting coins has been fun for me, and some day I hope to get a full collection of the Lincoln cents. They started in 1909. I get some coins for Christmas each year, mostly the ones I can't afford on my own right now. There are always a few that I put on my list each year. If you collect coins or are thinking about starting, I hope you have as much fun as I do at the coin shows. Give it a try and see. Which coins will you collect?

Washington State Quarters

One of the newest and most exciting ways to start collecting coins has just begun. The U.S. Government has begun a program in which each of the 50 states will design the back of a quarter dollar. Starting in 1999, five new quarters will be struck each year for 10 years.

The photo above on the left is the obverse (front) of the normal Washington Quarter. The photo above on the right is the obverse of the new Washington Quarter. As can be seen in the photos, the front of each quarter pictures George Washington, our first president. The photo on the right is one of the designs that was submitted in 1932 when the Washington Quarter was first struck. There are some changes to the front of the new quarters. One of the most interesting is that the date will be found on the back of the coin. How many coins have you ever seen with the date on the back? There are only a few coins ever struck at the United States Mint that had the date on the back of them. QUARTER DOLLAR, and UNITED STATES OF AMERICA, which are on the back of the Washington Quarters, are now on the front of these new quarters. E PLURIBUS UNUM is on the reverse of the new quarters.

The back of each coin will have the new designs for each state. Many states are having contests to pick the new design. So if you have artistic talent and your state hasn't already chosen a design, you might want to give it a try. Each year from 1999 to 2008, the Mint will provide five new state quarters. The order in which they will be done is the same order in which each state became a member of the United States. Delaware was the first state and Hawaii the last to become part of the United States. Normal Washington quarters will not be struck during these 10 years. Below is the reverse of the first five state quarters which were struck in 1999.

Now try and locate these quarters. There are a few different ways to do this. You can go to a coin store and buy the coins, but the best and most exciting part is that these quarters can be pulled from pocket change or you can get uncirculated coins from any bank. I would recommend finding the coins yourself because this is fun. You will notice that on each quarter on the front right-hand side, under "GOD WE TRUST," there is a small letter. It may be a 'P,' 'D,' or 'S.' This letter is called the mintmark and tells you which Mint the coin was struck in. 'P' stands for the Philadelphia Mint, 'D' stands for the Denver Mint, and 'S' stands for the San Francisco Mint. Coins struck at the Philadelphia Mint are mainly found on the East Coast, while coins struck from the Denver Mint are mainly found on the West Coast of the United States.

Coins struck at the San Francisco Mint are special struck coins made for proof sets. These coins have a mirror-like finish (you can see yourself in the coin). Dies that are used for proof coins are polished to give a shiny finish. The proof dies are only used to strike about 3,000 coins, but normal dies are used to strike about 1,000,000 coins. This way the dies do not wear out, and the coins have a strong design struck into them.

Proof sets are sold by coin dealers, or you can get them from the United States Mint directly. They are sealed in plastic containers and are not made to be used in change. They are made especially for collectors. You can also buy Mint sets of the new Washington Quarters. These are sold with the normal Mint sets for the year. The difference between a Mint set and a Proof set is that Mint sets contain coins struck at the Philadelphia and Denver Mints with normal dies. After the coins are struck, they are placed in the sets. By pulling the coins out after they are struck, the coins have no marks on them from being put into bags with thousands of other coins. Below is a part of the 1999 Mint set. The photo on the left shows the five 1999 state quarters that were struck at the Philadelphia Mint, and the photo to the right shows the cent, nickel, dime, and half dollar that were struck at the Denver Mint.

Normal Washington Quarters and the new state quarters are made of a metal called Clad coinage. The top layer is made of copper and nickel, while the inside is made of copper. The Mint will be making special Proof sets of the new quarters in which silver will be used. These sets will be available through the Mint and coin dealers.

The easiest way to start collecting these quarters is to find one of each state quarter regardless of the mintmark. Or maybe try for the P and D mintmarks of each state quarter. This will probably be the most common way to collect since both types of coins are available in regular change.

Once you decide whether you want to collect just one of each of the 50 state quarters or one each of the P and D mintmarks for each of the 50 quarters, you will need a place to store them. There are alot of different books, boards, and other ways to save your coins. There are boards that you can hang on your wall, books for storing one of each state, P and D mintmarks for each state, and P, D, and S mintmarks plus the silver proof coin for each state. There are also cases to hold the five different states struck in one year. Or you can get cases to hold a single coin struck from one state. There are many choices. Below on the left are some examples of a 1999 state quarter year set for holding one of each coin. On the right are two different 1999 state quarter sets for coins from both the Philadelphia and Denver Mints.

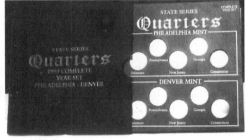

One of the nicest ways to collect just the 50 states is with a map with individual cutouts for each state. You can hang this on your wall and keep track of the coins you have and those you need. You just have to be careful with these, because as there is nothing covering the coins. This is also a great way to learn where each state is located, so it may help you to learn your geography for your school work.

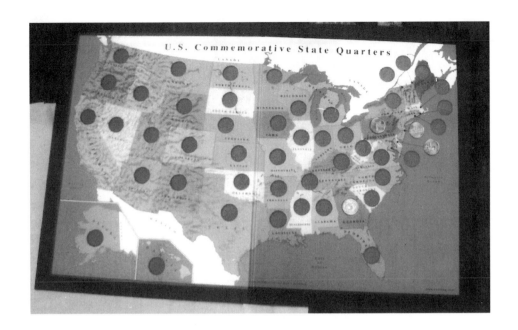

If you want to collect all 50 state coins and make sure your coins are well taken care of, you might consider using one of the albums. The great thing about these is that the front and back of the coin is protected by a plastic insert. The front and back of the coins can also be studied easily.

You can get a album that allows you to collect only what you want. For example, on the next page on the left is a book that holds one of each state. The book in the middle holds one of each state from both the Philadelphia and Denver Mints. The book on the right holds one of each state from the Philadelphia Mint, Denver Mint, Proof, and Silver Proof. The prices for the different holders and books range from $3.00 to about $25.00. You can buy them in many different places.

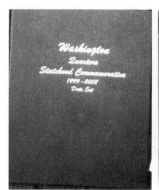 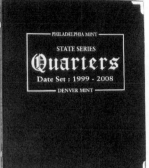 

The United States Mint has started a Web site for kids. The Web address is http://www.usmint.gov. Follow the directions to kids hip pocket change web site. You will find alot of interesting information here, including some interesting information about each state and a schedule when each state's coin will be available. If you still have questions or can't find any coin holders, you can email Brooklyn Gallery at info@brooklyngallery.com, and they will try to point you in the right direction.

The following page is a list of all 50 states. They are listed in the order in which they became part of the United States. This is the order in which the state quarter will be issued. Also listed is the state's capital, year it came into the United States, and other interesting facts.

Make sure you read the section in the book about handling and storing coins. Remember to only hold your coins by their edges, and do not touch your coins with dirty hands. Try not to breath on your coins. The best thing about this state quarter program is that you can collect at home looking through your pocket change. There are so many places to go and learn more about coins and so many types of coins to collect. It's a great hobby.

State	Capital	Statehood	Order	Nickname
Delaware	Dover	1787	1	First State, Diamond State
Pennsylvania	Harrisburg	1787	2	Keystone State
New Jersey	Trenton	1787	3	Garden State
Georgia	Atlanta	1788	4	The Empire State of the South
Connecticut	Hartford	1788	5	The Constitution State
Massachusetts	Boston	1788	6	The Bay State
Maryland	Annapolis	1788	7	Old Line State
South Carolina	Columbia	1788	8	Palmetto State
New Hampshire	Concord	1788	9	Live Free or Die
Virginia	Richmond	1788	10	Mother of Presidents
New York	Albany	1788	11	Empire State
North Carolina	Raleigh	1789	12	The Old North State
Rhode Island	Providence	1790	13	Little Rhody
Vermont	Montpelier	1791	14	The Green Mountain State
Kentucky	Frankfort	1792	15	The Bluegrass State
Tennessee	Nashville	1796	16	Volunteer State
Ohio	Columbus	1803	17	The Buckeye State
Louisiana	Baton Rouge	1812	18	The Pelican State
Indiana	Indianapolis	1816	19	The Hoosier State
Mississippi	Jackson	1817	20	The Magnolia State
Illinois	Springfield	1818	21	Prairie State
Alabama	Montgomery	1819	22	The Heart of Dixie
Maine	Augusta	1820	23	The Pine Tree State
Missouri	Jefferson City	1821	24	The Show Me State
Arkansas	Little Rock	1836	25	Land of Opportunity
Michigan	Lansing	1837	26	The Wolverine State
Florida	Tallahassee	1845	27	Sunshine State
Texas	Austin	1845	28	Lone Star State
Iowa	Des Moines	1846	29	Hawkeye State
Wisconsin	Madison	1848	30	The Badger State
California	Sacramento	1850	31	Golden State
Minnesota	St. Paul	1858	32	The Gopher State
Oregon	Salem	1859	33	The Beaver State
Kansas	Topeka	1861	34	The Sunflower State
West Virginia	Charleston	1863	35	Mountain State
Nevada	Carson City	1864	36	The Silver State
Nebraska	Lincoln	1867	37	The Cornhusker State
Colorado	Denver	1876	38	The Centennial State
North Dakota	Bismarck	1889	39	The Flickertail State
South Dakota	Pierre	1889	40	The Mount Rushmore State
Montana	Helena	1889	41	The Treasure State
Washington	Olympia	1889	42	The Evergreen State
Idaho	Boise	1890	43	Gem of Mountains
Wyoming	Cheyenne	1890	44	The Equality State
Utah	Salt Lake City	1896	45	The Beehive State
Oklahoma	Oklahoma City	1907	46	The Sooner State
New Mexico	Santa Fe	1912	47	Land of Enchantment
Arizona	Phoenix	1912	48	The Grand Canyon State
Alaska	Juneau	1959	49	North to the Future
Hawaii	Honolulu	1959	50	The Aloha State

Delaware

The state of Delaware was the first of the 13 original colonies to sign the Constitution on December 7, 1787. The name of the state comes from the bay and river on its eastern side. Delaware Bay and Delaware River were named for Lord De La Ware.

The reverse shows Caesar Rodney on horseback. Caesar Rodney was a famous patriot from the state of Delaware who served as a general in the Revolutionary War and was one of the signers of the Declaration of Independence. He was also Governor of the state of Delaware and a justice on Delaware's Supreme Court.

In the spring of 1776, the Continental Congress was meeting to discuss breaking away from British rule over the colonies. On July 2, 1776, the Congress was going to take a vote. At that time, there were two representatives from Delaware: Tom McKean who favored independence and George Reed who did not. Rodney made an 80-mile ride on horseback and arrived at Independence Hall with just minutes to spare to cast his vote for independence. This historic ride on horseback was voted by Delawareans to represent their state.

Pennsylvania

Founded by William Penn in 1681, the state was originally supposed to be named "Sylvania," which means woodlands. King Charles II of England suggested adding "Penn" in honor of William Penn's father, a great admiral. William Penn's "Great Law" protected life, liberty, and property through a jury trial. He also wrote the Charter of Privileges in 1701.

Pennsylvania hosted the Continental Congress in Philadelphia 1776 to sign the Declaration of Independence. The Federal Constitutional Convention was held in Philadelphia in 1787 to form a unified government. The Constitution of the United States was written here. Philadelphia was also the second capital of the United States. In 1792, the United States Mint in Philadelphia produced the first coins of the United States.

The reverse of the Pennsylvania state quarter shows a female figure representing the Commonwealth. The state's motto "VIRTUE, LIBERTY, and INDEPENDENCE" is to the right of the statue with an outline of the state of Pennsylvania in the background.

New Jersey

New Jersey was settled by the Dutch in the early 17th century. With New Jersey being between New York and Philadelphia, the two major cities of the colonies, many historic battles were fought in New Jersey during the American Revolution. This included Washington crossing the Delaware River during Christmas night to defeat the Hessian army. This historic crossing was chosen for the reverse of the New Jersey state quarter and is based on the 1851 painting by Emmanuel Leutze. The words "Crossroads of the Revolution" are printed under the design.

New Jersey was the third state to sign the Constitution on December 18, 1787. From June 30 to November 4, 1783, Princeton served as a temporary national capital, as did Trenton from November 1 to December 24, 1784. Thomas Edison invented the light bulb at his laboratory in New Jersey as well as many other inventions such as the alkaline storage battery and the phonograph. New Jersey is named after England's Isle of Jersey. The land was given in 1664 by the Duke of York to John Berkeley and Sir George Cartaret.

Georgia

Georgia was first inhabited by Cherokee and Creek Native Americans. In 1540 it was claimed by Hernando de Soto for Spain. In 1733, James E. Oglethorpe and a group of about 120 followers built a settlement on the Savannah River around Yamacraw Bluff.

Georgia is sometimes called the "Peach State," its nickname is "the Empire State of the South." Georgia is named after King George II of England who in 1732 approved of the charter to settle a colony in Georgia by Oglethorpe. The name was chosen by Mr. Oglethorpe.

Georgia was the fourth state to sign the Constitution and become a state. Eli Whitney invented the cotton gin in 1793, which separated cotton seeds from the fiber and revolutionized the cotton industry. Civil rights leader Dr. Martin Luther King Jr. was born in Georgia. The design of Georgia's state quarter is of a peach inside the outline of the state of Georgia. A banner reading the state's motto "Wisdom, Justice, Moderation" is draped on the outside with oak spring branches.

Connecticut

Connecticut was first claimed by a Dutch explorer, Adrian Block, in 1614. He called this "New Netherland" and established a fort and trading post in 1633. Block and his followers were driven out by English settlers who had migrated west from Massachusetts.

Settlers from Wethersfield, Windsor, and Hartford formed their own laws called the Fundamental Orders of Connecticut in 1639. This was the document that gave people the right to elect government officials. Governor John Winthrop in 1662 obtained a royal charter, making Connecticut an independent colony.

The name Connecticut comes from the Mohican words meaning "long river place." Connecticut's nickname is the "Constitution State," as it was the first state to establish laws to govern itself. Connecticut was the fifth state to sign the Constitution on January 9, 1788.

The design on the state quarter shows a white oak with the words "The Charter Oak" to the left. The 1662 British charter gave

Connecticut the right to govern itself and established the borders of the state. On October 31, 1687, Sir Edmund Andros, a British representative of King James II, tried to take the Charter of Connecticut.

At a meeting between Sir Andros and representatives of Connecticut, with the charter on a table between, the candles mysteriously went out. When they were relit, the Charter was missing.

The Charter had been taken by Captain Joseph Wadsworth, who hid it in a white oak on the property of the Wyllys family. Captain Wadsworth had saved Connecticut from returning to British rule.

Massachusetts

Massachusetts was the sixth state to join the Union on February 6, 1788. The design on this coin includes the words "The Bay State" which is the state's nickname, an outline of the state with a star showing its capital in Boston, and a figure of a Minuteman.

The Minuteman represents the volunteers who fought the British during the Revolutionary War. The name comes from the idea that they would be ready in a minute to fight for the freedom of this country.

Massachusetts gets its name from an Algonquian village that meant "place of big hills". The motto "The Bay State" originates from Massachusetts Bay, the area where the pilgrims first settled when the Mayflower first landed at Plymouth Rock in 1620.

Massachusetts is rich in history. The Boston Tea Party, Bunker Hill, the shot heard around the world, and Paul Revere are all represented by the patriotic Minuteman symbol.

Maryland

Maryland was the seventh state to join the Union on April 22, 1788. The design features the Maryland State House dome with oak leaf clusters on both sides. The state's motto, "The Old Line State" also appears.

The first European explorer to come here was Giovania da Veararano, an Italian explorer in the 1500s. In the 1600s, many English settlers came and settled in the Chesapeake Bay area to escape religious oppression and find new jobs.

Maryland got its nickname, the Old Line State, during the Revolutionary War when 400 soldiers fought against 10,000 British soldiers and helped General George Washington's army escape. The soldiers bravely earned Maryland its nickname.

Maryland was named after Queen Maria, the wife of King Charles I of England. The Star-Spangel Banner was written by Francis Scott Key at Fort McHenry.

South Carolina

South Carolina was the eighth state to join the Union on May 23, 1788. Featured are the Carolina Wren, a Palmetto tree, the state flower a yellow jasmine, and the state outline with a star indicating the state capital of Columbia. The state motto "The Palmetto State" is also printed.

South Carolina was first explored in the 16th century by the Spanish and French. They found native Americans consisting mainly of the Cherokee and Catabas Indians. The first permanent English settlement was established in 1670 near present-day Charleston and named after King Charles I. In 1760, Carolina was divided into North and South Carolina. During the Revolutionary War, many battles were fought in this region. With the invention of the cotton gin, cotton became a major crop and the state prospered.

South Carolina was the first state to succeed from the Union on December 20, 1860, in protest over the restrictions of free trade and the calls for stopping slavery. On April 12, 1861, the first shots of the Civil War were fired at Fort Sumter.

New Hampshire

New Hampshire became the ninth state on June 21, 1788. The main design consists of a profile view of the rock formation called The Old Man of the Mountain. The words "Old Man of the Mountain" the state motto "Live Free or Die", and nine stars representing the ninth state are seen.

New Hampshire was settled in 1623 by the English to establish a fishing colony for England.

New Hampshire is known as the Granite State because of the many mountains that cover the state. One of the most famous is the Old Man of the Mountain, which is a rock formation that resembles the profile of a man.

At the Battle of Bunker Hill, most of the soldiers were from New Hampshire, New Hampshire Captain John Paul Jones had many victories at sea to help the new colonies win their independence from England. New Hampshire was the most northern of the original 13 colonies.

Virginia

Virginia became the 10th state on June 25, 1788. Three 17th century ships are the featured design on this quarter. The design commemorates the Quadicentennil of the settlement of Jamestown (1607-2007). A quadricentennil is a 400th anniversary. This quarter will feature three separate dates: the 1788 date which represents the state's entrance into the Union, the 1607-2007 date, which represents the 400th anniversary, and the 2000 which is the date of issue.

Jamestown was the first permanent English settlement and represents the oldest continuous legislative body in this part of the world. In June of 1606, King James I and his crew chartered the "Virginia Company" to find a way to the Orient. Instead these settlers landed on Jamestown Island. The new settlers faced many difficulties, including disease, famine, and Indian attacks. However, with the leadership of Captain John Smith, the colony took root. The settlement began to prosper after Pocahantas married John Rolfe, which brought peace between the Indians and the settlers. The settlement then became a part of the Virginia colony in 1624 and was the capital of Virginia until 1698.

Sacagawea Dollar

The new dollar coin will be the first new coin of the millennium here in the United States. The coin has a gold-colored finish, which makes it easier to identify from the similar-sized quarter dollar. The coin is made of mostly copper and zinc and contains some nickel and manganese. By adding enough zinc to the copper, the coin appears golden in color. Although the coin is being called the gold dollar, there is no gold in this coin.

In 1997, Congress passed the United States Dollar Coin Act, which allowed the making of a coin that was gold in color, the same size as the Susan B. Anthony Dollar, and having an edge that could be distinguished from other coins. The Secretary of the Treasury's requirements for the new dollar were that the obverse contained the image of one or more women, that the image not be of a living person, and that the reverse must show an eagle.

The obverse design was created by Glenna Goodacre. Mrs. Goodacre used a real person as a model for the Sacagawea Dollar, Randy'L He-dow Teton. In 1998, the Mint requested Goodacre to submit a design for the new dollar coin. At the Institute of American Indian Arts Museum in Santa Fe, New Mexico, Mrs.

Goodacre asked if there were any young Shoshone women in the area. One of the employees was Miss Teton's mother, who showed Mrs. Goodacre pictures of her three daughters. Mrs. Goodacre contacted Miss Teton, who was 22 at the time, and did a sculptor of her image.

The reverse design was created by Thomas D. Rogers, Sr. It shows a soaring American bald eagle, the symbol of our nation. It is surrounded by 17 stars, which stand for the 17 states that existed in 1804 in our Union during the time of the Lewis and Clark expedition.

Sacagawea was a Shoshone Indian girl who was a guide for the Lewis and Clark expedition in 1805. Lewis and Clark were famous explorers who explored land west of the Mississippi for the young United States. These explorers opened the doors for the expansion of the United States to the Oregon Territory. But without the help of Sacagewea, this expedition would have been doomed.

The history of Sacagewea's life is incredible, as she is truly an American hero. Born into a Shoshone tribe and sister of a Shoshone chief named Cameahwait, she was captured at age 11 by a Hidatsa raiding party. She was later sold into slavery to the Mandan Sioux tribe who were living in Fort Mandan, North Dakota. She was then gambled away to a French-Canadian fur trader named Toussaint Charbonneau, who made her his wife.

At age 15, Sacagawea spoke several Indian languages. Lewis and Clarke hired Charbonneau for the skills of Sacagawea. Being a Shoshone, she would be helpful in obtaining horses, which were very important to the mission. But Sacagawea also knew about the land the expedition was traveling, parts of which was some of the most rugged parts of North America. She also taught them how to find edible plants and roots to eat.

At age 16, Sacagawea was pregnant when Lewis and Clark first met her. She gave birth to her son Jean Baptiste (nicknamed Pomp) in February of 1805, and in April of that year joined the expedition. When their boat overturned in the Missouri river, Sacagawea, with her son strapped to her back, saved Captain Clark's journals of the first year of the expedition, saving also a part of history.

More importantly, Sacagawea helped the expedition by serving as a translator, diplomat, and peace symbol to the native American Indians who they met. Her presence as a young mother helped the expedition avoid battle with Indians, whose land they passed through. Not a single member of the expedition was lost to a hostile action.

To help promote the new Sacagewea Dollar and celebrate the millennium, General Mills, the maker of the cereal Cheerios, will be adding a special prize to 10 million boxes of Cheerios. They will be placing 1 Sacagawea Dollar in every 2,000th box of Cheerios. In the other boxes, they will be placing a 2000 date Lincoln cent. A special prize certificate worth 100 Sacagewea Dollars will be placed in a limited number of boxes. Also, in July of 1999, twelve 22-karat gold versions of the new Sacagawea Dollar went into space on the space shuttle Columbia. This shuttle mission was the first to fly with a female commander, Eileen Collins. These coins were later placed into museums.

Modern Series of United States Coins

There are many types of coins you can collect. This section describes coins that are still being made at the United States Mint. These are the most commonly collected United States coins. The series are in order from cents through dollars.

You can collect any of these series from pocket change or with help from your family or friends, so have fun and enjoy this great hobby. Searching for coins in circulation can be like treasure hunting and is one of the best parts of coin collecting. Collecting the new Washington State Quarters is a great place to start collecting because all coins can be found in your pocket change.

When you start buying coins from coin shows or from stores, make sure you do your research first. Before you buy coins, go to shows or stores and look at the many different series. Find which coin series you like and that you can afford. If most of the coins in a series that you like are very expensive, save it for later. Plan a budget with your parents. If you find that many of the coins in a series are not easy to find, then you might want to start with another series. It is best to start with a series that is readily available and that you can choose from many different types of the coins.

One of the easiest ways to begin is to pick a modern series that was only made for a short time such as the Eisenhower Dollars or the Susan B. Anthony Dollars. These series are readily available at coin shows or stores for an inexpensive price. You can also obtain all dates and mintmarks of these series in a short amount of time.

Other series that were made at the United States Mint and are enjoyed by many collectors are in the next section. These include Indian cents, Buffalo nickel, Mercury Dime, Morgan Dollars, and others. Only series that are affordable for the beginner are covered in this book. When you are ready for other series, make sure you do the research first by reading books and studying the coins.

Description of Information Given for Each Series.

Photographs: Photographs showing the obverse and reverse of the coin.
Designer: Person who designed the obverse and reverse of the coin.
Years Struck: The years in which the coins were struck.
Mints: The Mints where the coins were struck.
History: History of the creation, design chosen, and other facts regarding the coin. Any changes in the design, metal used, or other changes.
Unusual Coins: These are coins that were made by accident and are highly collected by the public.
Collecting: Gives different ways to collect a series. Tells what grades are best to search for and what years are more rare and expensive.
Key Dates: These are the harder dates to find and obtain. This is usually because of low mintage of that date. It also could be because few coins were saved for that year.
Interesting Facts: Facts about the coin or the person shown on the coin.

LINCOLN CENTS

Designer: Obverse and Wheat Back Reverse: Victor D. Brenner
             Memorial Reverse: Frank Gasparo
Years Struck: 1909 to present
Mints: Philadelphia, Denver, San Francisco
Mintmark Location:
1909 to present - below date

History: The obverse of the coin shows a picture of President Lincoln, our 16th president. This coin was created to celebrate the 100th anniversary of President Lincoln's birth. President Lincoln was born in Kentucky in 1809. The Lincoln cent is the first United States coin made for circulation that had the picture of a president. A reverse containing the wheat stalks on the side was used from 1909 to 1958. The reverse was changed to celebrate the 150th anniversary of this great president in 1959, the new reverse has a picture of the Lincoln Memorial.

In 1943, the metal of the Lincoln cent was changed to steel with a zinc coat (grey colored). This was done because bronze, which was used to make the cents, was needed for bullets for World War II. In 1944, the metal was changed back to bronze (brown colored).

Unusual coins: In 1943 when the cent was changed to steel, some blank planchets that were left over from the 1942 cents accidentlly were struck with the 1943 dies. There are also some steel cents that were struck with 1944 dies. Both of these are extremely rare and valuable. One 1943D bronze cent sold for $84,000.

Collecting: Modern coins can be found in pocket change. Some wheat back reverses dated before 1959 can still be found in circulation. Most early Lincoln cents can be purchased at coin shows in low grade for a reasonable price. Early perfect Lincoln cents can be expensive.

Key Dates: 1909-S, 1909-S VDB, 1914-D, 1922, 1926-S

1909 VDB - designer's initials   1909 - without VDB
bottom of reverse

 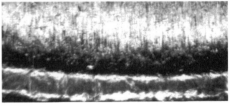

Facts about President Lincoln: Abraham   Lincoln's portrait is found on the one cent coin (penny) of the United States. Our 16th president was considered by some to be one of our greatest presidents. Lincoln came from a simple beginning; he was born in a log cabin in Kentucky. He had little schooling but did alot of reading and learned everything he could.

He worked hard and became a lawyer. Mr. Lincoln was opposed to slavery and he made many speeches, letting his feelings be known. He ran for the Presidency of the United States in 1860 and won. Almost immediately, South Carolina and other southern states that were for slavery began to leave the Union (United States of America). On April 12, 1861, the Civil War began when soldiers from the southern states (called the Confederacy) fired on Union soldiers at Fort Sumter in South Carolina. This was a terrible war, but Lincoln knew it must be fought to save the future of Democracy and end slavery in the states.

Finally on April 9, 1865, General Robert E. Lee surrendered to General Ulysses S. Grant. However, President Lincoln was not able to bring the Union states and Confederate states back together because 5 days after the end of the war, he was shot and killed by John Wilkes Booth. So, even though the war was ended, there was still alot of hatred between the two sides.

One of President Lincoln's most famous speeches was the Gettysburg Address. In this speech, he stated "this nation, under God shall have a new birth of freedom; and that government of the people, by the people, and for the people shall not perish from the earth." He also started the move to make all men equal, independent of color.

JEFFERSON NICKEL

Designer:	Felix Schlag	
Years Struck:	1938 to present	
Mints Struck:	Philadelphia, Denver, San Francisco	

Mintmark Location:

1938-1942	1942-1945	1968-present
1946-1964	Silver war time nickel	

History: In 1938, the Treasury Department wanted to replace the Buffalo nickel with a new design. A competition was held to pick the design. The obverse design had to be of our second president, Thomas Jefferson, and the reverse of Jefferson's house, Monticello. The prize was $1,000. In World War II, nickel was needed for bullets. In 1942, the metal was changed from nickel to silver. Both types of metal were used for the nickel in 1942. To tell the difference, the mintmark was moved from the right side of Monticello to over the dome. The silver metal was used from 1942 to 1945. All silver nickels have the mintmark above the dome. After World War II, in 1946, the metal was changed back to nickel, and the mintmark was moved back to the right side of Monticello. In 1968, the mintmark was moved to the obverse below the date.

Collecting: The nice part of this series is that many of the coins can be found in circulation, especially from 1965 to date. Most of the earlier coins can be found for reasonable prices at coin shows or stores. An uncirculated set of the entire series is a good way to collect this series.

For the best struck coins, check the steps of Monticello on the reverse. Nickel is a very hard metal. More pressure is needed to strike these coins because nickel is so hard. Many early dated Jefferson nickels are weakly struck. This can best be seen on the steps of the Monticello on the reverse. If there are six full steps, then this coin was fully struck and is known as a "Full Step." Most Jefferson nickel proofs are fully struck and have six steps. This is mainly because proofs are struck twice to increase the detail. For some dates, especially before 1970, it is rare to find business strikes, which have six full steps; these are worth more. A complete set of Jefferson nickels with at least five steps would be a nice challenge.

Key Dates: 1939-D, 1939-S, 1942-D
Striking for Jefferson Nickels

Full step (6 steps)	5-1/2 steps	No steps
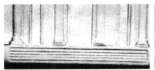		

Facts about President Jefferson: Thomas Jefferson was our third President. Jefferson was not a very good public speaker, but he was truly one of the greatest writers of his time. His letters and articles brought him great fame in America. Because of his writing skills, he was appointed to write the Declaration of Independence.

President Jefferson also invented the American money system that we still use today. Jefferson was the founder of the Republican party. (This party's name later changed to the Democratic party, which is the same Democratic party we have today.)

Jefferson believed that the people of the nation should and could govern themselves. He also believed all children should be educated in schools. During his presidency he purchased the Louisiana territory. This territory more than doubled the size of the United States.

Jefferson served two terms as president. He may have been elected again but did not want to appear to be a dictator and believed no president should serve more than two terms. He also succeeded in keeping the power of the government in the hands of the people.

After his presidency, he retired to his home in Virgina. This beautiful home was called Monticello and is pictured on the back side of the Jefferson nickel.

During Jefferson's later years, he continued to help our nation grow. He died on July 4, 1826, which was the same day our second president John Adams died. It was also exactly 50 years to the day after the signing of the Declaration of Independence.

ROOSEVELT DIME

Designer: John Sinnock
Years Struck: 1946 to present
Mints Struck: Philadelphia, Denver, San Francisco, West Point
Mintmark Location:
1946 - 1964 - left of torch   1968 - present - above date

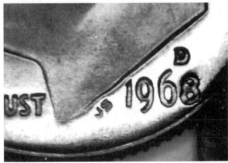

History: With the death of President Roosevelt in 1945, the Treasury Department wanted to put his portrait on a coin. The dime was chosen and the Mint Chief Engraver John Sinnock created the obverse and reverse designs. The obverse is of President Roosevelt and the reverse is of a torch with an olive branch around it symbolizing peace after World War II. Silver was used for the dimes from 1946 through 1964. Because of the high cost of silver in 1964, the alloy was changed in 1965 to a clad or sandwich combination of copper in the middle, and cupro nickel on the outside. From 1946 to 1964, the mintmark is located to the lower left of the torch. From 1965 to 1967, no mintmark was used. In 1968, the mintmark was moved to the front of the coin over the date.

Collecting: This is a good set to start with. Many of the coins from 1965 to date can still be found in circulation. Coins from 1946 to 1964 are not expensive to purchase. There are many coins available at shows and stores. Take your time and buy coins that you like. Coins that are spotless and white are recommended.

Key Dates: 1949-S, 1949, 1950-S

Facts about President Roosevelt: Franklin Roosevelt was our 32nd president. He was born into a famous family. He was related to many of the earlier presidents. Roosevelt was involved in politics from the start. During World War I, he was the Assistant Secretary of the Navy. Unfortunately, he became ill with polio and lost the use of his legs. But this did not stop him. He became governor of New York in 1926 and served during the late 1920s and early 1930s. He did such a good job that in 1932 he was elected President. The Great Depression was still affecting the country and Roosevelt took action. Roosevelt lobbied Congress to pass many laws to help the many people who lost their homes and savings during the Depression. Roosevelt also started many social programs during his "New Deal Administration" to help the common man. Many of these programs provided work to people with no jobs. During this time, much of the nation's roads, bridges, clearing away of trees, and building of dams was done. Roosevelt was also still President in 1939 when World War II began. Even though he tried to stay out of the war, he was given no choice when the Japanese bombed Pearl Harbor on December 7, 1941. Roosevelt and many other allied leaders made plans to defeat the Axis powers. Before the war could be won, Roosevelt became ill and died. Roosevelt had served four terms as President. He was the only President to serve more than two terms. Roosevelt believed it was important for him not to quit because the country was dealing with such difficult times.

WASHINGTON QUARTER

Designer: John Flanagan, Jack L. Ahr
Years Struck: 1932 to 1999
Mints Struck: Philadelphia, Denver, San Francisco
Mintmark Location:

1932 - 1954   1968 - present
Below wreath on reverse   To right of ribbon on obverse

History: The obverse of the coin shows a picture of President George Washington, our first president. This coin was created to celebrate the 200th anniversary of President Washington's birth. In 1931, the Treasury Department had a contest. The winner was Laura Gardin Fraser, a distinguished sculptor. But Secretary of the Treasury Andrew Mellon refused to allow Miss Fraser to design the new quarter because she was a woman. Mr. Mellon picked the design of John Flanagan to be used for the quarter. The reverse design is an eagle on a group of arrows above a wreath. Several changes were made over time to strengthen the design and improve the strike. In 1965, with a shortage of silver, the metal was changed from silver to a clad or sandwich combination of copper middle to a copper nickel outside. To celebrate the bicentennial of the United States in 1976, a new reverse design was used for the quarter and was used for all quarters made in 1975 and 1976. This featured a drummer boy next to a torch surrounded by 13 stars. All quarters made in these two years are dated "1776-1976." The normal reverse was used again in 1977.

Collecting: This is a fun series to collect. Coins from 1965 to date can be found in pocket change. Coins from 1944 to 1964 can be bought in MS63 grade for an average of $4.00. This is a nice grade to collect these uncirculated coins as there is sharp detail and there are a lot of coins to choose from for this time period. Earlier coins before 1944 are more expensive for some date and mintmarks. Collect these dates in grades of very fine to extra fine. Always look for coins that have no marks and no color.

Key Dates: 1932-D, 1932-S, 1934-D, 1936-D, 1935-D

Facts about President Washington: A portrait of George Washington is found on the United States quarter. Washington is considered to be the Father of our Country. He was elected to be our first president in 1789. He served two terms as our president. Many people wanted him to continue a third term, but he believed it was important to step down and allow others to lead this great country.

Washington was born a farmer. When he was 21, he began his military life. During his military career, others realized what a great leader he was based on his ability to inspire his troops.

After the colonies won their independence from England in 1776, many of the colonies considered themselves independent states and there was fear that they might start fighting among themselves. So in 1787, most of the important leaders in America held a meeting called the Constitutional Congress.

Washington was the chairman of the convention. The Constitution of the United States was drawn up at the meeting and is still the same laws that govern today.

These great men also nominated George Washington to be the President, and he received every vote.

During his presidency, he tried to be the leader of all the people. He also tried to avoid being a dictator but knew that the government could not last unless it could enforce its laws on the individuals and the government.

He established what the office of the presidency should be. He kept our young country together and provided a plan for it to grow.

KENNEDY HALF DOLLAR

Designer: Gilroy Roberts, Frank Gasparro, Seth Huntington
Years Struck: 1964 to present
Mints Struck: Philadelphia, Denver, San Francisco
Mintmark Location
1964 - Below right leg of eagle   1968 - present - Below
bust

History: After the assassination of President Kennedy in 1963, the half dollar was changed to contain his portrait on the obverse. The presidential coat of arms was used for the reverse of the coin and was designed by Frank Gasparro. The obverse was designed by Mint Chief Engraver Gilroy Roberts. Mr. Roberts used the design on President Kennedy's inaugural medal to help get the coin done on time. In 1965, because of the rising cost of silver, the half dollar was changed from silver to a silver clad, or sandwich combination of silver and copper. This was used until 1971, when the metal was changed to a copper nickel clad of a copper center with copper nickel used on the outside. To celebrate the bicentennial of the United States, the reverse design was changed for the quarter, half dollar, and dollar. The reverse design for the half dollar is Independence Hall from Philadelphia, which was designed by Seth Huntington. Coins struck in these three series during 1975 and 1976 contained the doubled date "1776-1976." There are no quarters, halves, or dollars dated 1975.

Collecting: Almost any coin from this series can be still found in circulation, including a silver 1964 and 1964-D. This would be an exciting series to attempt to collect all dates and mintmarks from coins found in circulation. Your parents, relatives, or grandparents might be helpful with some of the 1960 coins if you need them. If you want to collect Mint State coins, MS64 to MS65 graded coins can be bought for an average of $1.00. Look for coins with no marks and original white coloring.

Key Dates: 1970-D

Facts about President Kennedy: The half dollar of the United States bears the image of John F. Kennedy. Our 35th President was the youngest person ever to become president.

President Kennedy served in the Navy during World War II. After the war, he began his political career. He was first elected to Congress, then to the Senate. He was elected President in 1961. During his presidency, he developed the Peace Corps to help people in poorer countries. Kennedy was also a leader for civil rights in our country. When he was president, there was still segregation in our country. He worked toward ending this separation of citizens. Unfortunately, his term as president ended suddenly. He was assassinated in Dallas, Texas, on November 22, 1963. He was one of our country's most beloved presidents.

SUSAN B. ANTHONY DOLLAR

Designer: Frank Gasparro
Years Struck: 1979 to 1981, 1999
Mints Struck: Philadelphia, Denver, San Francisco
Mintmark Location:
1979 - 1981 - Left of bust

History: The obverse is of Susan B. Anthony, a leader in women's rights. This was the first coin in which an image of a woman was used on a United States coin. The reverse is the same as was used on the reverse of the Eisenhower Dollars, which was created to celebrate the first landing on the moon.

One problem was that this coin was very close in size to the Washington quarter and would sometimes be confused with it. In 1999, the Susan B. Anthony Dollar was again struck for a single year. This was done because the Treasury vaults ran out of these dollars and more were needed. The new Sacagawea Dollar was not ready yet, so it was decided to make more Susan

74

B. Anthony Dollars.

Unusual Coins: Two different style 'S' mintmarks were used for both 1979 and 1981 proofs struck at the San Francisco Mint. The 1979 Type I block 'S' is much more common than the Type II clear S. The 1979 Type II clear S is also worth about $55.00 compared to $5.00 for the Type I blocked S. In 1981, there was a Type I block S and a Type II clear S, with the 1981 Type II clear S being worth about $90.00 compared to the $5.00 for the Type I.. There are two different types of date styles used for the 1979 Philadelphia struck coins. There is the 1979 Far Date and the 1979 Near Date. The near date is rarer and has a wider rim than the Far Date.

Collecting: This is one of the simplest series to put together. These coins can also still be found in circulation. They are being used by vending companies in candy and soda machines. Around 800 million of these were struck. Most were put into the Treasury vaults. They have been slowly used over the past 18 years.

The new 1999 Susan B. Anthony Dollar was released into circulation in October 1999 and can be found in circulation. It was only struck for 1 year because the supply of dollars in the Treasury vaults ran out and the new Sacagawea Dollar was not scheduled to be released until the year 2000.

Key Dates: 1979S Clear S, 1981S Clear S

Other Collectible Series

In the previous section, only the United States coin series currently being made were discussed. There are many other series that you can collect and enjoy. This section covers some of the more popular series that are collected and are in a price range of a beginner collector.

Older coin series such as the Large Cents, Half Cents, and other series made in the early 19th century can be expensive and not recommended for beginners. These series are very popular and collected by an experienced group of collectors who have studied and learned a great deal about these older coins.

Before you collect some of these older or more expensive series, you have to learn more about grading, how rare coins are, interest level, and other factors that determine the price and value of a coin. Before you spend alot of money, you need to make sure you understand what you are buying.

There are certain dates for coins in the currently made series that are expensive. Remember that the Lincoln cent was first made in 1909. A 1909 with an 'S' mintmark and the V.D.B. initials on the back can cost more than $300.00 in low grades. Only 484,000 of these were made, which is a small number, making these coins rare for Lincoln cents. So learning more about a coin series is needed whenever you plan to spend money on a coin, whether it's a coin made today or 200 years ago.

The series covered in this section are some of the more popular series, which means there are alot of collectors interested in them and in trying to collect them. Collecting a popular series is good because when you want to sell your coins, it is much easier to find dealers and collectors who are interested. But, higher interest can also mean higher prices when you are buying. There are other series such as the Two cent and Three cent nickels that do not have alot of interest by collectors, which also means cheaper prices for these coins.

You will not find most of these series covered in this section in pocket change, but your parents or grandparents might have some saved from when they were young.

Description of Information Given for Each Series.
Photographs: Photographs showing the obverse and reverse of the coin. The photos are the same size as the coin.
Designer: Person who designed the obverse and reverse of the coin
Years Struck: The years in which the coins were struck.
Mints: Mints where coins were struck.
History: History of the creation, design chosen, and other facts regarding the coin. Any changes in the design, metal used, or other changes.
Collecting: Provides different ways to collect a series. Tells what grades are best to search for and what years are more rare and expensive.
Key Dates: These are the harder dates to find and obtain. This is usually because of low mintage of that date. It also could be caused by few coins being saved for that year.

INDIAN CENTS

Designer: James B. Longacre
Years Struck: 1859 to 1909
Mints Struck: Philadelphia, San Francisco
History: Because of the weakness of the strike of the Flying Eagle cent, in 1859, Chief Engraver James Longacre changed the design of the cent. He chose for the new obverse an "Indian Head." This is believed to be the face of Venus Accroupie, a Greek-Roman god with an Indian headdress. The reverse has a laurel wreath. In 1860, the reverse was changed to an oak wreath with a shield on top. In 1864, an 'L,' for Longacre, was added to the ribbon on the obverse. With a shortage of nickel in 1864, the metal of the cent was changed to bronze and used until 1909.

Collecting: This is a very popular series for 19th century collectors. Many collectors like the artistic design, others enjoy the challenge of a series made over a 50-year period. This coin was made during a period of great change in our country; the west was being expanded, and new inventions were created that changed the entire way people traveled and did things. You will not find these coins in circulation, but your grandparents might have saved some. There are several ways to collect this series. Low-grade coins from most years can be bought for a reasonable price except for a few dates such as 1877, which is expensive even in low grade. It is suggested that you start with 1880 to 1909 in grades of EF-40, the average price will be about $8.00 per coin and the coin will be in a grade in which you can see a lot of detail. Coins before 1880 can be expensive in this grade. If you want to put a nice Mint State set together, start with coins from 1880 to 1909 in grades of MS63 Red and Brown. These coins have an average price of about $25.00. Indian Head cents are red when they are created and can change color to brown. Red coins are worth more than brown. Red-brown Indian cents still have the nice red color, but have changed slightly to brown. These are much cheaper, but just as nice. Look around to see what you enjoy.

Key Dates: 1877, 1864L, 1909-S, 1872, 1871

FLYING EAGLE CENTS

Designer: James B. Longacre
Years Struck: 1857 to 1858
Mints Struck: Philadelphia
History: In 1856, because of the rising price of copper, the cost of making the Large and Half cents was more than the face value of the coin. Congress decided to make a new cent. The Mint Chief Engraver, James B. Longacre, used an eagle for the obverse and a wreath for the reverse. The wreath contained the main staple production of the United States at that time. A few hundred 1856 Flying Eagle cents were made for Congressmen. These 1856 cents were not made for the general public and are considered very rare today. In 1857 the coins were produced for the public. People gathered around the block at the Mint and at banks to trade their old Large and Half cents for the new cents. Many of these new cents were saved by people. This started a whole new generation of coin collectors just like today with the new Washington state quarters.

Collecting: Heavily collected with the Indian cents. Low-grade coins can be bought cheaply. Nice uncirculated coins can be expensive. Coin folders and albums usually have the Flying Eagle cent and the Indian cent together as part of a set.
Key Date: 1856

BUFFALO NICKEL

Designer: James Earle Fraser
Years Struck: 1913 through 1938
Mints Struck: Philadelphia, Denver, San Francisco
History: In 1911, Treasury Secretary Franklin MacVeagh wanted to change the design for the nickel. James Earle Fraser was asked to create and submit designs. For the obverse of the coins, Fraser chose a portrait that was a composite of three native American Indian Chiefs: Iron Tail (Custer's opponent at the Little Big Horn), Two Moons, and John Big Tree. On the reverse, Fraser chose an American bison, Black Diamond, who was living at the Central Park Zoo in New York. Two different reverse designs were used in 1913. On the first design used, known as Type I, it was found that FIVE CENTS at the bottom of the coin wore too quickly. The reverse was changed to put FIVE CENTS below the height of the mound; these are known as Type II and were used for the rest of the series.

Unusual coins: In 1937, one of the Denver dies was polished on the reverse, removing the front right leg of the Buffalo. This is known as the 3-1/2 leg variety and is very valuable. This coin

80

can still be found at coin shows and stores. The same type of polishing can be found from dies used for 1913-D, 1917-D, 1927-D, and 1936-D. More of the leg is polished away on the 1937-D.

Collecting: This is one of the more popular series to collect. You will not find these coins in circulation, but check with your grandparents. They might have saved some from when they were young. A low-grade complete set is not very hard to assemble. If you are looking for a Mint State set, start with coins from 1930 to 1938. Coins from 1920 through 1929 can be much more difficult to find and can be very expensive in high grade, especially coins from the Denver and San Francisco Mints. Many of the coins struck in the 1920s are also weakly struck.

Key Dates: 1926-S, 1924-S, 1927-S, 1925-S, 1921-S, 1918-S

MERCURY DIME

Designer: Adolph A. Weinman
Years Struck: 1916 to 1945
History: The same design was used for the Barber dime, quarter, and half dollar. In 1916, the Mint wanted to replace all three with new designs. The Treasury Department had a competition in which Adolph Weinman's design won for both the dime and half dollar. For the obverse of the dime, Mr. Weinman used a portrait of Elsia Stevens wearing a winged cap. Many people mistakenly thought the head on the Mercury dime was an image of Hermes or Mercury in Greek folklore. This is why this coin

is called the Mercury dime. The reverse design is a Roman fasces, an axe bound with a group of rods, which was surrounded by greenery. This design was probably symbolic of the United States stance on liberty and justice in World War I.

Collecting: Mercury dimes are an undervalued and under collected series. This is good for the collector who enjoys this series. Less demand means cheaper prices and more coins to choose from. The entire series can be put together with the average price of about $1.00. Many of the Mint State coins before 1930 are rare and expensive. A good place to start with this series is to collect each date and mintmark between 1934 and 1945 at a grade of MS63. The average price of these coins will be about $10.00 and you will have nice uncirculated examples. Try to look for spotless coins.

There are two horizontal bands on the center of the Roman fasces on the reverse. These bands are directly opposite the highest point on the obverse and are often weakly struck. When there is complete separation between the lower and upper middle band, this is known as "Full Bands" or "FB." If only part of the bands is separated, it is called "Split Bands," and if there is no separation, it is called "Flat Bands". Mercury dimes with full bands are worth much more.

Key Dates: 1916-D, 1921, 1921-D, 1926-S, 1925-D

| Full Bands | Split Bands | Flat Bands |

FRANKLIN HALF DOLLAR

Designer: John Sinnock
Years Struck: 1948 through 1963
Mints Struck: Philadelphia, Denver

History: The obverse is of Benjamin Franklin, with the Liberty Bell used as the main design for the reverse. Created at the request of Mint Director Nellie Tayloe Ross, this was the Mint Chief Engraver John Sinnock's last work, which he completed only a few weeks before he died. The reverse design of the Liberty Bell is from the sketch of John Frederick Lewis, which was also used for the Sesquicentennial Commemorative half dollar made in 1926.

Collecting: This series is not heavily collected, which is good for those who wish to collect it. Less demand means cheaper prices and more coins to choose from. This is a nice short series, which makes it easier to complete. These coins cannot be found in circulation, but you might want to check with your parents or grandparents to see if they have any saved. The best grade to collect these coins is MS63 to MS64. Circulated coins graded extra fine cost about $4.00. MS63 coins cost an average of about $11.00 for coins between 1952 and 1963 and about an average of $25 for coins between 1948 and 1951. It is worth spending a little extra to get a real nice uncirculated coin that you will not have to upgrade. Make sure you pick nice white coins that have no marks and no color or toning.

Coins with good strikes will have "Full Bell Lines" (also called

FBL) at the bottom of the Liberty Bell on the reverse. Even for proofs that are struck twice, it is hard to find full lines across the bottom, especially on the left side of the bell.

Key Dates: 1949-S, 1949, 1951-S, 1952-S

Full Bell Lines   Not Full Bell Lines

LIBERTY WALKING HALF DOLLAR

Designer: Adolph A. Weinman
Years Struck: 1916 through 1947
Mints Struck: Philadelphia, Denver, San Francisco
History: Adolph Weinman designed both the Mercury Dime and Liberty Walking Half Dollar. The United States Treasury Department had a competition in 1916 to make a new dime, quarter, and half dollar. Mr. Weinman won a prize and a commission to do both a new dime and half dollar design. The obverse design is Miss Liberty with an American flag around her. In 1916, World War I was in progress in Europe. Perhaps this design was chosen to show American unity. She is carrying a bundle of oak and laurel branches in her left arm. The cap on

Miss Liberty's head is the same style as used on the Mercury dime. The reverse shows an eagle with a Mountain Pine to the left.

Collecting: The short set is much easier and a good place to start for this series. This set contains each date and mintmark from 1941 through 1947. If you are completing a low grade set of the entire series most coins can be bought for about $4.00 per coin, with the exception of a few dates such as 1921 and 1921-D. For a mint state set, many of the coins struck in the 1920s are hard to find and expensive. If you are really interested in a mint state set, work on the short set first in mint state. Many of these coins are common in uncirculated grades, so you have a wide choice to pick the coins you like.

Strike is important for mint state coins. On the obverse look at the gown around the hip, left hand, and face of Miss Liberty. On the reverse, look at the breast feathers of the eagle.

Key Dates: 1921-S, 1921-D, 1919-D, 1919-S, 1917-S, 1923-S

EISENHOWER DOLLAR

Designer: Frank Gasparro, Dennis R. Williams
Years Struck: 1971 through 1978
Mints Struck: Philadelphia, Denver, San Francisco
History: The obverse is Dwight D. Eisenhower, our 20th president from 1952 to 1960, and one of the greatest leaders of

the United States in the 20th century. He was the Supreme Allied Commander in World War II. The reverse represents the landing on the moon, our greatest technological achievement in the 20th century. President Eisenhower was also part of this achievement as he signed the bill into law that created NASA. To celebrate the bicentennial in 1976, the reverse of the quarter, half dollar, and dollar were changed and used for one year. For the Eisenhower Dollar, the Liberty Bell over the moon was used.

Collecting: This series is very easy to assemble for all dates for all three mints. These coins can be obtained for a small price at coin shows or stores. Because all coins are inexpensive, it is suggested that you collect this series in high grade. Also with so many coins available to choose from, take your time and choose the best pieces with no marks or toning.

Key Dates: All dates and mintmarks are relatively easy to obtain.

PEACE DOLLAR

Designer: Anthony De Francisci
Years Struck: 1921 through 1935
Mints Struck: Philadelphia, Denver, San Francisco
History: The Peace Dollar was made to commemorate the signing of the peace treaty at the end of World War I. The Commission of Fine Arts held a contest for the design. Only eight sculptors were invited to submit designs for the coinage.

Mr. De Francisci won. For the obverse, he used a composite of Miss Liberty and a sketch of his wife Teresa. The reverse design is of an eagle holding an olive branch with rays of sunlight in the background.

Unusual Coins: In 1964, the Mint was considering using the Peace Dollar again for circulation coinage. A total of 316,076 Peace Dollars dated 1964 were created. One was given to President Johnson by Mint Director Eva Adams and is believed to be in the library of President Johnson and someday will go to the Smithsonian. Plans for the Peace Dollar in 1964 were abandoned and all but a few were melted. It is believed that besides the specimen given to President Johnson, about 20 were taken out of the Denver Mint through employees of the Mint. If any of these 1964D Peace Dollars were found, they would be taken by the Secret Service and melted. Only coins officially released by the Mint are legal coins.

Collecting: Morgan Dollars are much more popular and collected more than Peace Dollars. This is a short series, but these coins can be expensive. In grades of very fine, all coins can be obtained at an average of $12.00 with the exception of the 1928 and 1934-S. Some uncirculated coins can be purchased for around $25.00, but most are more expensive. This series is not recommended for a beginner. Many coins are weakly struck, especially the hair on the obverse and the eagle's feathers on the reverse. Save this series until you can afford a little more. If you are interested in starting with this series, first collect the Philadelphia struck coins as they are less expensive.

Key Dates: 1921, 1924-S, 1927-D, 1928, 1934-S, 1935-S

MORGAN DOLLAR

Designer: George T. Morgan

Years Struck: 1878 through 1904 and in 1921

Mints Struck: Philadelphia, San Francisco, Carson City, New Orleans

History: The Morgan Dollar series was created mainly because of politics, greed, and the silver mine owners. More than 550 million Morgan Dollars were struck between 1878 and 1904. About 490 million of these were put into Treasury vaults, and only about 70 million went into circulation and were used. This means that 90 percent of the Morgan Dollars struck were never used.

The silver dollar is a heavy coin that was not used regularly by the public. In 1873, Congress stopped the production of the silver dollar in the United States. Congress authorized the creation of a Trade Dollar, but this was used for trade with other countries, mainly China. During the 1870s, Germany put a lot of silver on the market. Also in the United States, many new silver mines were opening in the west. This meant that the price of silver fell. The silver miners wanted to keep the price of silver high and force the Mint to only buy silver here in the United States. In 1878, with the help of Congressman Richard Bland and Senator William Allison, Congress passed a law that forced the Mint to buy 2 million to 4 million dollars a month in silver for a new silver dollar. The silver miners were paid in gold. By 1893, the Treasury department was almost out of gold, and this caused more than 400 banks to close. In 1904, coinage of the Morgan Dollar was stopped. They were struck again for 1 year in 1921.

Unusual Coins: None known

Collecting: This is an extremely popular series, mainly because of the design and availibility of the coin. Many coins can be found in mint state condition. This is because most of the coins struck were put into Treasury vaults. In 1964, many of these coins were sold to the public.

Key Dates: 1893-S, 1892-S, 1895, 1895-O, 1884-S, 1889-CC, 1903-S

Grading Coins

Coin grading is an important part of coin collecting. It is the most important thing that you need to learn if you really want to collect coins. The grading of coins has to do with how much wear or circulation the coin has received. More use leads to the coin's design becoming more worn. This in turn affects the coin's condition and value. Always remember the grade of a coin is based on personal opinion. If someone tells you it is one grade and you disagree, then you should not buy the coin. There are no experts. Each person grades differently and you must learn to grade and trust your own experience that you learn through examining many different coins.

There are many books that can help you learn how to grade coins. Two of the standard books are: <u>Photograde</u>, and <u>Official ANA Grading Standards for United States Coins</u>. These books are helpful tools, but the best way to learn how to grade coins is to examine various graded coins and see the differences on the coin.

It is important when examining coins to use the right lighting and magnification. Four to eight power magnification should be fine. Ten power or more should be used to study small differences in a coin and to determine grading. When examining a coin, hold the coin on its edges between your fingertips. Make sure a soft padded surface is beneath the coin in case it is dropped. Tilt the coin at an angle so that the light reflects from the coin's surface to your eye. By tilting or turning the coin, different parts of the coin can be observed. Try not to breathe on coins, especially copper coins, and do not talk while holding one in front of you.

The grade of a coin reflects the condition. Wear, contact marks, hairlines, scratches, nicks, color, luster, and eye appeal all contribute to the grade of a coin. The grade of a coin is one of the most important factors in establishing the value of a coin. Grades for coins made for circulation are from 0 through 70, with 70 being perfect. Coins that show no signs of wear are assigned a grade of 60 through 70 and are known as Uncirculated (Unc) or Mint State (MS). The following are some of the general terms and standards used in the hobby to describe the grade of the coin. These descriptions are general; the exact descriptions will differ from series to series.

The basic circulated grades are given first. Lincoln cents are shown as an example for each grade.

The design of the coin is the main image. For example, on the Lincoln cent, the obverse design is the image of President Lincoln. The lettering or legend are usually the lettering around the rim of the coin. The date is the date the coin was struck, which is usually at the bottom of the front of the coin. The highest point on the coin is the part of the design that is raised the highest above the surface of the coin and usually will begin to wear first.

The most important thing to learn about grading is that the more coins you study, the better you will be at telling what grade a coin is. Study as many coins as you can and compare coins to see differences.

General Descriptions of Circulated Grades

About Good (AG-3) - Very heavily worn. Design worn smooth, but the general outline is still visible. Most of letters around the rim are only partially visible. The date is worn but visible, allowing you to tell which year the coin was struck.

Good (G-4) - Heavily worn. Most of the design is worn flat, but major parts of the design are visible. Letters around rim are worn but mostly visible. Date is fully visible.

Very Good (VG-8) - Well worn. Major features of design flat, but visible. Letters around rim are clear.

Fine (F-12) - Moderate to considerable wear. Entire design is bold, with some higher points visible.

Very Fine (VF-20) - Moderate wear on high points of design. Major details are clear.

Extremely Fine (EF-40) - Only slight wear. Major features of design are sharp and well defined.

About Uncirculated (AU-50) -   Traces of light wear seen on most of the highest points of the design.

Mint State coins show no signs of wear. The grade of a Mint State coin is based on the coin's luster, number of bag marks, scuff marks, location of marks, color of the coin, and eye appeal. Remember, what grade one dealer or collector might consider a coin will usually vary from another dealer. It is always best to learn to grade yourself. The following are some general descriptions of Mint State coins:

MS-60 - Many possible large contact marks, hairlines or scuff marks throughout. Possible rim nicks. Poor eye appeal. Surfaces may be dull or spotted. Dull luster.

MS-63 - Only a few scattered large contact marks in prime areas, numerous small contact marks. A few small scattered patches of hairlines in secondary areas. Several possible scuff marks in fields and on the design. Attractive eye appeal. Surfaces have some original color. Luster may be slightly impaired.

MS-65 - One or two large contact marks in prime areas or a few small contact marks. One or two small patches of hairlines. A few scuff marks on high points of design. Very pleasing eye appeal. Surfaces have full original color or tone. Attractive average luster throughout.

MS-70 - Perfect coin. Outstanding eye appeal. Surfaces bright with lustrous original color. Very attractive blazing luster.

Buying Coins

The best way to start a collection is to find coins in circulation. This offers an inexpensive and exciting way to enjoy this hobby.

As you continue to collect coins, there may be some coins that you can't find or coins that don't look as nice as others you have. You may then want to try to buy the coin you are looking for.

If you are considering buying coins, you should first plan with your parents how much you are going to spend and you must know what you want. The value of a coin can change depending on how it looks. If a coin is marked, scratched, or cleaned, it will be worth far less. How strong the strike of the design is also important for many series. This means how much detail shows up on the coin. When you look at a Lincoln cent, some coins show more detail than others.

In addition, in some series such as the Buffalo nickel series, many of the 1920 to 1929 coins are weakly struck. A strongly struck Buffalo nickel during this time, especially for the Denver and San Francisco struck coins, are worth far more. When Buffalo nickels are first struck they are white. Over time, they can tone or change color to a goldish color. This can be caused from air or being handled by people. If you are collecting this series, what color do you want your collection? It is better to look at many Buffalo nickels and decide what you like. This is true for any series. It is also important to learn more about the series that you want to collect, what color are the coins normally and what color can they change to, and what years have weak strikes. Weak strikes happen when not enough pressure is used in the Coining Press, when the coins are struck. It also could happen if the master hub or master die becomes worn down from use.

Look around at coin shows and stores and see what you like. If a series that you like is found at many dealer's tables, then you will have many coins to choose from and can choose the best for your collection. If the coins are hard to find, they are also probably expensive and you should not try to start there. Again, after you pick a series that you want to collect, buy a book on the series, which will tell you what to look for in grading, color, and availability. There are books on almost any series. If you just go out and buy coins before you research, you might have to replace the coins later with better coins. It is better to wait, learn, and buy the coin that you really want.

Make a "Want List" of what coins you are looking for and set a price for what you want to pay for them. When at a coin show, do not buy the first coin you see that you need. Different coin dealers will charge different prices for the same coin. It is best to shop around, find the coin you want, and find the best price. Many times, coin dealers mark the price of the coin on the holders of the coins. Many will come down in price if you ask them nicely what their best price would be for the coin.

Always remember that when you are buying coins, be careful if someone wants to sell you a coin for a lot less than it's worth. There is probably something wrong with the coin. Be careful and talk to your parents about coins you want to buy.

Collecting Die Varieties

To make a coin, we use a tool called a 'die.' The die has the image of the coin on it. We need two dies to strike a coin: one for the obverse and one for the reverse. The coins are struck in a machine called a Coining Press. The pair of obverse and reverse dies are placed above and below the coin. The coin is struck by the dies with thousands of pounds of pressure.

To make the dies, there are a whole bunch of steps that the Mint has to take. These steps will be covered in another book. Sometimes during the die making process, mistakes can be made. These mistakes can make the die look different from other dies. These are known as die varieties. There are many collectors who collect these die varieties. Some types of die varieties are very valuable. Some types are very common during certain years. Below are some examples of different types of die varieties.

A doubled die is when there are two or more images on a die. There are many different reasons how these doubled dies can be created. Below is a picture of a 1955 Lincoln cent with very dramatic doubling seen all around the coin. This is one of the more dramatic doubled dies for the Lincoln cent series. In perfect condition, this coin can be worth around $15,000.00. Imagine paying five cents for this coin and selling it for alot of money. There are thousands of the doubled dies on 20th century coins. Many are minor and worth only a little, but imagine finding a monster like the 1955.

There are other types of doubling that are not valuable. In these cases, the doubling happens when the coin is being struck in the coining press or sometimes when the die wears down. It is important if you want to collect doubled dies to be able to know the difference between a true doubled die and other types of doubling.

A repunched date is when the date was punched into the die more than once. We only see repunched dates on coins that were made before 1909. Before 1909, the date was struck into each die by a Mint person who used a hammer and a date punch. Sometimes he wanted to get a deeper impression into the die or thought it was too high or low. Many of these repunched dates only show minor signs of extra digits. Some are very dramatic and are valuable. Below on the left is an 1864 Two cent piece with repunching. Look at the second 18 above the normal 18; see how high it is. On the right is a photo of an 1864 Two cent piece, which was punched four times showing four different images of the digits.

A misplaced date is the same as a repunched date, but the repunched digits are much farther away. Sometimes by accident, the digits of the date were punched into the denticles below the date or the design of the coin above the date. There are alot of reasons this could happen. Mainly, it is thought that it was caused by inexperienced Mint employees or by misjudgement. Remember the area in which the date is struck is only one-quarter of an inch wide and one-tenth of an inch high. Misplaced dates happened on almost all coin series before 1909. There are no misplaced dates found on coins after 1908 because the Mint changed the way it made dies and no longer struck the date into the die by hand. There are 400 misplaced dates known and new ones being found all the time. Below on the left is an 1870 Indian cent with a bold 0 in the denticles. On the right is an 1847 five dollar gold piece with a bold 1 seen in the neck.

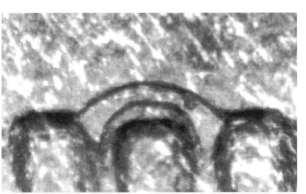
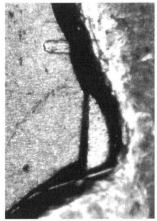

One of the rarest types of die varieties and sometimes the most valuable is an overdate. An overdate is a coin that shows two dates from different years. Let's first show what an overdate looks like. The photo below on the left is of an 1887 three cent nickel on which you can see the shape of a 6 under the 7. This working die was first struck with an 1886 date punch, then struck over with an 1887 date punch. The photo below on the right is of an 1918-D Buffalo nickel that shows a 7 underneath the 8.

There are roughly 200 overdates for all series. Most of these are for 19th century coinage. There are fewer than 10 overdates known for 20th century coinage. Overdates are one of the more collected and enjoyed type of die varieties.

A mintmark is used to identify which Mint a coin was struck. Up until around 1990, the mintmark was struck into each die by a Mint employee with a hammer and a punch with the mintmark at the end. If the Mint employee thought the first punch was too soft, too high, or too low, then he might strike the mintmark again into the die.

A repunched mintmark is a coin that shows two or more mintmarks punched into it. These are common for 20th century coinage, especially for Lincoln cents. There are more than a thousand repunched mintmarks known for the Lincoln cents alone. Some of the more dramatic repunched mintmarks can be very valuable.

In the photo below on the left, a totally separated D can be seen on this 1956D Lincoln cent. The photo on the right is of a 1942D Jefferson Nickel, in which the D is punched over a horizontal D.

An over mintmark is a coin that shows two or more different lettered mintmarks. The photo below on the left shows a 1944D Lincoln cent with an obvious S underneath the D mintmark. The center photo shows a closeup of the 1944D/S cent. The photo below on the right shows a 1938D Buffalo nickel with an obvious S underneath the D mintmark.

Over mintmarks are rare with about 50 known for all series. These are highly collected and sought after.

Collecting Error Coins

A die variety is when something happens to the die to make it look different from other dies. Every coin struck with that die shows the difference. An error occurs when something happens to the coin when the coin is being struck.

Let's start with the basics. A blank piece of metal (also known as a planchet) is fed into the Coining Press. An obverse die and a reverse die are in the Coining Press above and below the coin. Thousands of pounds of pressure are used to strike the image of the dies into the planchet.

What happens if the planchet is not fed between the dies properly? Half of the planchet is between the dies, and the other half is not. This is called an off center and some examples are shown below. On the left is a Lincoln cent which is 25% off center; the middle photo shows a Lincoln cent that is 50% off center, and the right photo shows a Lincoln cent that is 75% off center.

There are many types of coin errors and there are many books that have been written about them. The next page shows some different types of error so you get an idea of what they look like.

Struck over Different Denomination

Clipped Planchet

Double Struck

Chain Strike

Capped Die

Brockage

Flip Over Double Struck

Folded Edge Struck

Collecting Foreign Coins

Collecting foreign coins can also be fun. There are many different ways to collect foreign coins. You can collect one from each country or just collect coins from one country. However you like.

One of the nice things about foreign coins is that they are usually readily available and affordable. Foreign coins, even older ones, can be much cheaper than United States coins from the same time frame. The most popular and easiest foreign coins to collect are from Mexico, Canada, and England.

Foreign coins can come in many sizes and shapes. On the next page you can see a Turkish coin with a hole in the center. During the early part of our country's history, the U.S. Mint were thinking about different shapes that might be used, one of the shapes considered was a coin with a hole in the center.

Just like in the United States, the images used on foreign coins are famous people, history, places in that country, or perhaps something important. For example, on the top of the next page, we first see a coin used by the Vatican. On the front of the coin is Pope Paul II. England uses the images of its kings and queens on many of its coinage. Queen Elizabeth II is on many of the coins used today. Elk is an important animal in Canada, and is portrayed on Canada's coinage. A dragon, which is a well-known symbol in China, is used on China's coinage.

Coin shows are usually a good place to find coin dealers who specialize in foreign coins. In addition there is usually an abundance of coins to look through.

1995 Vatican Coinage Pope Paul II	England Queen Elizabeth II	Canada 1969

Turkey 1948	Jamaica 1989	Algeria 1964

Norway 1964	Switzerland 1968	China 1914

Collecting Hobo Nickels

Hobo nickels are Buffalo nickels that were modified through carving by the homeless during the early 20th century. They were traded for meals, a place to sleep, a ride, or other favors. Often they were carved of loved ones to remember better times.

These unique pieces of metal combine the fields of numismatics, art, and history. The Buffalo nickel is one of the most loved of all the coins in the United States. Its design is true Americana. The years of its reign, 1913 to 1938, take us through some of the most remarkable periods in the history of the United States, including the first World War, the Roaring 20s, the Great Depression, Prohibition -- times we must not forget.

Each of the original hobo nickels is unique as they were hand carved, using the design either of the Indian or buffalo as a base and changing it so that it represents another design. The Indian has been changed to represent clowns, Amish men, women, other Indians, friends, loved ones, and self-portraits. The buffalo has been changed to donkeys, men with packs on their backs, and elephants.

If they could talk Hobo nickels would have stories to tell about the men and women who created them and who struggled during that very harsh period in our country. On the next page, we see some examples of hobo nickels.

There is a coin club that studies hobo nickels, The Original Hobo Nickel Society. If you are curious and want more information, you may contact this society. An application is in the back of this book.

Examples of Original Hobo Nickels

Collecting Ancient Coins

Ancient coins are another way to collect coins. The great thing about ancient coins is that you can see what was important in that country or empire when the coin was made.

A good place to look at ancient coins is in a museum. Museums show and teach us about our past. Coins were an important part of previous civilizations and continue to be today just as important.

The following were written with the help of Robert Hoge, the curator at the American Numismatic Association Museum. The photographs on the following pages are courtesy of the ANA.

The first coin shown was made around 561-546 B.C. in the Lydian Kingdom, during the time of Croeus (Kroisos). The Lydian kings were probably the world's first minters of coinage (650 B.C.). It is a silver 1/2 stater made at the Sardes mint. Part of the first bi-metallic coinage, also used by the Persians. Because the primitive equipment that was used to make these coins, they are not perfectly round.

The coin at the top of the next page was made around 449-413 B.C. in Athens Greece. It is called a silver tetradrachm and was the primary coinage of Athens' "Golden Age." The most common classical Greek issue is often called "owls." Athens was the only Greek city with its own silver supply; its coins became widely accepted in trade.

The next coin was made around 336-323 B.C. in the Macedonian Kingdom. The front of the coin has a picture of Alexander III ("The Great"). The coin is a silver tetradrachm and was struck at the Pella or Thebes mint. Alexander adopted the Athenian coinage system's standard for his own, which was struck in dozens of mints and was used world wide throughout his empire.

This coin was made around 280-276 B.C. in the Roman Republic. It is part of the Aes Grave series of coinage struck at the Rome Mint and is called a bronze quadrans. The large cast Republican coppers display marks of their values. The Romans only began to produce coinage some 300 years after its introduction elsewhere.

The following coin was made between 123-88 B.C. in the Parthian Kingdom. A picture of Mithradates II is on the front. This coin is called a silver drachm and made at the Ecbatana Mint. The Partian empire was the great rival of Rome until about the 3rd century A.D. The Parthians ruled an enormous empire, and continued the Greek system of denominations and legends.

The coin below was made between 54-68 A.D. and shows the Roman Emporer Nero. It is called a gold aureus and was made at the Rome Mint. This coin was issued after the great fire and is thought to show Nero's great statue of himself. Many millions of coins were minted under the Roman empire, from a variety of mints scattered through the provinces.

The coin at the top of the next page was made in Judaea between 132-135 A.D. during the 2nd Revolt against Rome. It is called a silver denarius or zuz (1/4 shekel) and was made at the Jerusalem mint. Bar Kochba's (Kosiba) issues, overstruck on Roman coins. The Jewish people enjoyed only a brief period of independence when they were able to strike their own coins.

The coin below was made between 518-527 A.D. in the Byzantine Empire. The front has a picture of Justin I. The coin is called a gold solidus or nomisma and was made at the Constantinople mint. This was part of the common gold coinage that dominated the Greek--parent of the word "numismatics."

The following coin was made in China between 618-627 A.D. during the Tang Dynasty, Gao Zu. It is copper "cash," Kai Yuan Tong Bao issue. A major coinage that standardized the four character legend. Such square-holed coppers were cast with substantially no change, other than the words, for more than 2,000 years.

111

Conclusion

In the summer of 1999, Ron Volpe requested me to write this book. Ron has many kids which come into his store looking for a book on getting started on coin collecting.

As a child, I began coin collecting through boy scouts while earning a merit badge. I was fascinated by old coins of our country. My interest in coins was also pushed by my passion in American history which our coinage played a great part. The more I learned about our coins, the more I enjoyed collecting them.

By writing articles, books, or just doing a presentation on a subject, it is important to first learn all you can about the subject matter, so that you understand, and then can share the correct information with others. The sharing of knowledge among collectors is one of key goals of coin collecting today. Find a subject or series that you enjoy, learn more and write an article about it. Its a great way to meet new people and have discussions on a subject.

I have written 15 books to date. Most of these were focused on history, die varieties and the great stories behind a series. Writing a book for kids offered a new challenge for me. I asked my daugther Kelsey, to help me with this project, because I wanted the book to be written with a kid's viewpoint. Kelsey's fourth grade class read the book and gave me some helpful feedback.

I learned a great deal and had alot of fun writing this book. I hope each of you enjoy reading and learning from this book, and enjoy this great hobby.

Have fun, Kevin Flynn.

Terms and Definitions

<u>Design on the Coin</u>

Obverse - Front of the coin.

Reverse - Back of the coin.

Date - The year the coin was struck which is required to be on the coin.

Design - The main image on the coin. For example, on the Lincoln cent the main image on the obverse would be the image of President Lincoln. On the reverse, it would be the Lincoln Memorial.

Device - same as the main design on the coin.

Legend - The words "UNITED STATES OF AMERICA", which is required to be on all coins.

Motto - The words "E PLURIBUS UNUM", which is required to be on all coins today.

Mintmark - Tells which Mint a coin was struck at, for example: P stands for Philadelphia, D for Denver, and S for San Francisco.

Rim - This is the outer raised portion of the coin. It helps protect the design from wear.

Denticles - Small raised bumps that are used on the inside of the rim on some earlier series such as the Indian cents.

Field - The flat surface of the coin.

Designer's Initials - Initials of the person who created the design for the coin.

<u>General Terms:</u>

Relief - The design on the coin which is raised or above the surface of the coin.

Incused - The design on the coin which has been impressed into or below the surface of the coin.

Business strike - A coin which is made for general use and circulation.

Proof strike - Specially made coin for collectors. These coins are not made for circulation. They usually have a mirror field, and a strong strike.

Mintage - The number of coins struck in a year for a single denomination.

Series - All coins from the same denomination and same design. For example, the Lincoln cents is a series.

Denomination - The numerical name of a series which is the value of the coin. Example: Two cent pieces has a denomination of two cents.

Mint State - A business strike coin which has never been used in circulation.

Uncirculated - A coin which shows no sign of wear.

Circulated - A coin which shows signs of wear from usage.

Commerative Coin - A coin which is not used for business. It is made to celebrate a person or event.

Planchet - The blank piece of metal which is struck in the coining press with the design of the coin.

Counterfeit - A fake coin which was made outside the Mint, or by changing a real coin.

Cleaning - Removing dirt or something from the coin or altering the coin by cleaning or washing the surface of the coin. This process can damage the coin and decrease its value.

Die Varieties:

Die variety - A working die which is different from other working dies of the same denomination and date because of something which happened during the creation of the die. This could be as simple as the date position, die crack, or this could be doubling, repunching, or a number of things which would make it different from other dies.

Repunched Date - Working die in which the date was punched into the die more than one time showing more than one set of digits.

Misplaced Date - Similar to a repunched date, but the digits are punched into the denticles, design or some place not near the date.

Overdate - A working die which has two dates of different years punched into it.

Repunched Mintmark - Working die in which the mintmark has been punched in more than one time.

Over Mintmark - Working die which has the mintmarks of two different Mints punched into it.

Doubled Die - A working die which the design or letters have become doubled during the die creation.

Die crack - If the die cracks when it was being used in the coining press. There will be a crack in the die which will show up as a raised crack on the coin. Not seen often on coins today, very common on coins struck in the 19th century.

Die scratch - If the engraver or person taking care of the dies is trying to clean the dies to remove something on the die, he would polish the die with an abrasive. This could cause the die to become scratched.

114

RECOMMENDED READINGS

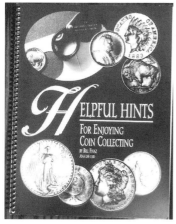

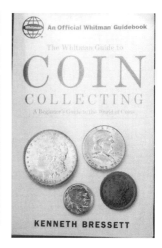

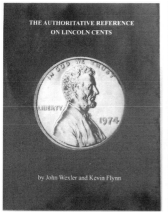

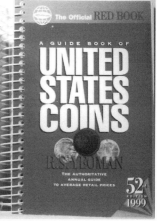

Magazines and newspapers:

Coin World - Weekly newspaper, usually available in coin shops. Subscriptions are available from Coin World, P.O. Box 150, Sidney OH 45365.

Numismatic News - Weekly newspaper, usually available in coin shops. Subscriptions available from Numismatic News, 700 E State St, Iola, WI 54990.

Books - General

Helpful Hints for Enjoying Coin Collecting, by Bill Fivaz, NLG. A very useful book for the novice collector from one of the most respected experts in the hobby.

Walter Breen's Complete Encyclopedia of U.S. and Colonial Coins, by Walter Breen. Explores the history, top varieties for each series.

Walter Breen's Complete Encyclopedia of U.S. and Colonial Proofs, by Walter Breen. Detailed study of all proof coins struck at the Mint.

A Guide Book of United States Coins (The Red Book). The most widely used reference and pricing guide used in the hobby.

Official ANA Grading Standards for United States Coins. A detailed grading book for all series.

Photograde. A detailed grading book for all series.

The Basics of Collecting Money. by Coin World. A introduction into coin collecting.

The U.S. Mint and Coinage. by Don Taxay. A excellent study and reference on the history of the United States Mint and how coins were produced.

BIBLIOGRAPHY

American Numismatic Association, Official A.N.A. Grading Standards For United States Coins, 1987

Breen, Walter. Walter Breen's Complete Encyclopedia of U.S. and Colonial Coins. New York, New York: Doubleday, 1988.

Bressett, Kenneth, The Whitman Guide to Coin Collecting, A Beginner's Guide to the World of Coins, 1999

Flynn, Kevin. Getting Your Two Cents Worth. Kevin Flynn, 1994.

Flynn, Kevin. A Collector's Guide to Misplaced Dates, 1997

Flynn, Kevin and John Wexler. The Authoritative Reference on Lincoln Cents, 1996

Flynn, Kevin John Wexler, Bill Crawford, The Authoritative Reference on Eisenhower Dollars, 1998

Flynn, Kevin Edward Fletcher, The Authoritative Reference on Three Cent Nickels, 1999

Flynn, Kevin, Morgan Dollar Overdates, Over Mintmarks, Misplaced Dates and Clashed E Reverses, 1998.

Flynn, Kevin, John Wexler, Ron Pope, Treasure Hunting Buffalo Nickels, 1999.

Flynn, Kevin, John Wexler, Treasure Hunting Mercury Dimes, 1999.

Flynn, Kevin, Bill VanNote, Treasure Hunting Liberty Head Nickels, 1999

Fivaz, Bill, Helpful Hints For Enjoying Coin Collecting, 1999

Fivaz, Bill and J.T. Stanton. The Cherrypickers' Guide to Rare Die Varieties. Third Edition. Wolfeboro, NH: Bowers & Merena Galleries, Inc., 1994.

Rudy, James, Photograde, 1995

Taxy, Don. The U.S. Mint and Coinage ARCO Publishing Company 1966

Wexler, John. The Encyclopedia of Doubled Dies, Volume 1, 1981

Wexler, John. The Encyclopedia of Doubled Dies, Volume 2, 1981

Wexler, John. The Lincoln Cent Doubled Die. Newbury Park, CA: Devine Printing Co., 1984

Wexler, John and Tom Miller. The RPM Book, Newbury Park, CA: Devine Printing Co., 1983

Wexler, John, Kevin Flynn. The Best of The Washington Quarter Doubled Die Varieties, 1999

Wexler, John and Brian Allen. The Complete Guide to Lincoln Cent Mistmark Varieties, JT Stanton, 1999

Yeoman, R.S. and Kenneth Bressett, ed. A Guide Book of United States Coins, 51st Edition, Racine, WI: Wextren Publishing Company, Inc., 1998

The National Collectors Association of
Die Doubling Membership Application

Name_____ Tel. No._____

Address_____

City_____

State__ Zip Code+4____ email address _____

Membership Rates (Please Check All That Apply)
New____ Renewal_____
Regular Membership $ 25.00 ____
Young Numismatic $ 10.00 ____
(under 17 years of age) D.O.B.
Date of Birth_____ Signature of Parent or Gardian_____
Outside U.S. (Canada) $ 9.00 ____ (For Postage Fees)
Other Countries, contact us

Total enclosed $ _____

Please Tell Us What Your Interest Are:
( ) **Doubled Dies** ( ) **RPMs and OMMs** ( ) **RPDs** ( )
MPDs ( ) **Other**_____

I collect the Following Denominations:
19th Century Coins____ 20th Century Coins
Cents _____ Nickels _____ Dimes _____ Quarters _____
Halves _____ Dollars___Foreign _____ Other _____
Please list club you are affiliated with and Positions that you
hold or held:

_____

_____

I was referred to **NCADD** by: _____
Make check payable to NCADD, Mail application and check
to:**Whaden Curtis, P.O. Box 109, East White Plains, NY**
10604-0109

ANA MEMBERSHIP APPLICATION
818 North Cascade Ave
Colorady Springs, CO 80903-3279

Junior Membership Dues:
  (17 years old and younger) - $11.00

Name _____

Date and Year of Birth _____

Address _____

City _____ State ____ Zipcode ____

I agree to abide by the American Numismatic Association bylaws and Code of Ethics which require the publication of each applicant's name and state.

[ ] Check here if you DO NOT want your name and address forwarded to the ANA Represenative in your area.

[ ] Check here if you would like your name provided to companies with offers we feel may interest you.

_____
Signature of Applicant

_____
Signature of Parent or Guardian

Send payment of $11.00 to American Numismatic Association

818 North Cascade Ave   Colorado Springs, CO 80903-3279

HOBO NICKEL MEMBERSHIP APPLICATION

Please check which membership you are applying for

[ ] 5 years $40.00   [ ] 3 years $25.00
[ ] 1 year $10.00   [ ] Life $250.00
[ ] Youth under 19 $5.00   [ ] Association $5.00 per year

Name: _____

Street_____

City_____, State_____ ZipCode_____

Date of Birth: ___/___/___

Moniker (Nickname):_____

   I agree to abide by the Society's Code of Ethics

Signature:_____

Sponsor: Bill Fivaz

Checks payable to: The Original Hobo Nickel Society
Send to: OHNS, P.O. Box 54583, Cincinnati, OH 45254-0583

Benefits:
1. Newsletter - BO TALES, published three times a year, plus an auction catalog.
2. Hobo Nickel Authenication Service
3. Educate numismatists and general public about ORIGINAL Hobo nickels, and the difference between them and modern reproductions.